Egyptian Gods

A Captivating Guide to Atum, Horus, Seth, Isis, Anubis, Ra, Thoth, Sekhmet, Geb, Hathor and Other Gods and Goddesses of Ancient Egypt

© Copyright 2020

The contents of this book may not be reproduced, duplicated, or transmitted without direct written permission from the author.

Under no circumstances will any legal responsibility or blame be held against the publisher for any reparation, damages, or monetary loss due to the information herein, either directly or indirectly.

Legal Notice:

This book is copyright protected. This is only for personal use. You cannot amend, distribute, sell, use, quote, or paraphrase any part of the content within this book without the consent of the author.

Disclaimer Notice:

Please note the information within this document is for educational and entertainment purposes only. Every attempt has been made to provide accurate, up to date, and reliable information. No warranties of any kind are expressed or implied. Readers acknowledge that the author is not engaging in the rendering of legal, financial, medical, or professional advice. The content of this book has been derived from various sources. Please consult a licensed professional before attempting any techniques outlined in this book.

By reading this document, the reader agrees that under no circumstances is the author responsible for any losses, direct or indirect, which are incurred because of the use of the information within this document, including, but not limited to, —errors, omissions, or inaccuracies.

Free Bonus from Captivating History (Available for a Limited time)

Hi History Lovers!

Now you have a chance to join our exclusive history list so you can get your first history ebook for free as well as discounts and a potential to get more history books for free! Simply visit the link below to join.

Captivatinghistory.com/ebook

Also, make sure to follow us on Facebook, Twitter and Youtube by searching for Captivating History.

Contents

FREE BONUS FROM CAPTIVATING HISTORY (AVAILABLE FOR A LIMITED TIME) 1
INTRODUCTION 4
TIMELINE OF ANCIENT EGYPT 8
AMEN (AMUN, AMON, AMMON) 11
ANUBIS (ANPU, INPW) 18
ATEN (ATON) 24
ATUM (TUM, TEM, ATEM, TEMU) 32
BASTET (BAST, BOUBASTIS, PASHT) 34
THE BOOK OF THE DEAD AND OTHER FUNERARY TEXTS 37
THE FOUR SONS OF HORUS 42
GEB (SEB, KEB, KEBB, GEBB) 44
HAPY (2; ALSO HAPI) 46
HATHOR 49
HORUS (HOR, HER, HERU, HAR) 53
IMHOTEP (IMOUTHES) 57
ISIS 61
KHNUM (CHNUM) 71
KHONSU (KHONS, CHONS) 73
MAAT (MA'AT, MA'ET, MAYET) 76
NEFERTEM (NEFERTUM) 78
NEITH (NEIT) 79

NEPHTHYS (NEBT-HET)	81
NUN (NOUN, NU)	83
THE OGDOAD OF HERMOPOLIS	85
OSIRIS	87
PTAH	94
RA (RE, PRE)	96
SERAPIS (SARAPIS, USERHAPI)	99
SET (SETH, SUTEKH)	102
SOBEK (SUCHOS)	105
THOTH	107
THE TUAT (DUAT)	111
BIBLIOGRAPHY	122

Introduction

It is tempting to see ancient Egyptian religion as something relatively static, with a single pantheon whose nature and activities did not change throughout the three-thousand-year span of the Dynastic Period. However, nothing could be further from the truth. Throughout Egyptian history, we see that gods who had once been favored were set aside or had their roles altered in order to make way for gods whose cults became more popular, while political changes, such as the conquest of Egypt by Alexander the Great, ushered in cultural and religious exchanges that both affected native Egyptian religious practices and also had an impact on the religious beliefs of Greece and Rome.

Fluidity was built into the structure of Egyptian religion itself. Many gods and goddesses had special relationships with other deities, often taking on aspects of those gods, such that a new, syncretized deity was created. We see this especially with the god Amen and the goddess Bastet. Amen's association with the sun god, Ra, created the syncretized deity Amen-Ra, and in this guise, Amen became the supreme deity of Egypt during the New Kingdom. Bastet, on the other hand, was not combined with a second deity but rather was seen to be the calm, affectionate avatar of the lion-headed goddess Sekhmet, who once went on a rampage and tried to kill all humankind. Sekhmet, in turn, was considered to be a violent manifestation of the cow-headed goddess, Hathor.

Syncretization was not the only way in which relationships were established or changed between and among Egyptian deities. For example, it sometimes can be difficult to establish which deity was the consort or child of which other god or goddess, since these groupings could shift depending on location and time period. For example, the god Khnum, who had his major cult centers in southern Egypt near the source of the Nile, was variously made the husband of the goddesses Satis, Menhit, and Neith, while the god Khonsu was worshiped as the son of Amen and Mut in southern Egypt, as the son of Ptah and Sekhmet in the north, or as the son of Hathor and Sobek in the Temple of Kom Ombo in central Egypt.

The importance of the family bond to ancient Egyptians is reflected in their preference for making collections of deities that represent family groupings. For example, the Heliopolitan Ennead (Nine Gods) represented four generations of the same family. More commonly, however, these groupings were of a single nuclear family of two parents and one child, usually referred to as a "triad." Although a temple might be dedicated to a single god such as Horus, that temple did not neglect to include both the god's consort and son or daughter although, as mentioned above, exactly which deities were grouped into which triads might vary depending on the historical period and location.

There are multiple ancient Egyptian creation myths, and which creation story a particular person accepted as true might depend on where they were from. For example, the major religious centers of Hermopolis, Thebes, and Memphis each had their own creation myth, and although some deities, such as Thoth, cross over from one cosmogony to the other, these tales are largely independent of one another. The three cities mentioned above were all large and important, but status was not necessary in order for a place to have its own creator god and creation myth. We see this with the ram-headed god Khnum, whose main cult centers were far from the seats of power, and who was considered to be the creator of the universe by the people who worshiped him in his shrines on the island of Elephantine and at Esna.

Because the pharaohs were deemed to be the sons of a deity (variously Horus the Younger or Amen-Ra, depending on the historical period), Egyptian religion was closely allied with politics. The pharaoh had the power to create and endow temples for the worship of the gods, and a pharaoh's particular religious enthusiasms could cause shifts in national religious beliefs and practices. We see these kinds of changes especially during the New Kingdom. For example, when Pharaoh Ahmose I defeated the invading Hyksos, who had taken over Egypt, he claimed that his victory was the result of Amen's favor. Pharaohs thereafter declared themselves the sons of Amen-Ra. This caused a surge in the popularity of Amen's cult, for which the vast temple complex at Karnak was constructed. Similarly, during the reign of the Ptolemies, interest in the goddess Isis increased the number of devotees to her cult, which spread beyond the boundaries of Egypt into Greece and Rome.

Pharaohs could also change (or at least attempt to change) religious practice by fiat. Pharaoh Akhenaten is perhaps the best known for this, having declared traditional worship banned in favor of his own monotheistic system that centered on the sun god Aten. Akhenaten's heresy was heavily resented by his people and did not outlast his own regime; his reforms were reversed by his son, Tutankhamun.

Changes instituted by other monarchs had considerably more staying power, however. This was particularly true of Ptolemy I's creation of the new deity Serapis. Serapis was considered to be the consort of Isis and was a syncretization of the god Osiris and the Apis bull. He had some Greek characteristics and was an attempt on the part of the Greek pharaoh to create commonalities between Greeks and Egyptians living under his rule.

Because the Egyptian pantheon is vast, even if one leaves out the syncretized deities, it is not possible for this volume to present a comprehensive overview of ancient Egyptian religion and myth. Instead, only a select number of deities and concepts are discussed here. Some of these are more well-known deities, while others might not be as familiar to modern readers. However, this book still offers a fascinating glimpse into ancient Egyptian religion and culture and the richness that was life in ancient Egypt.

Timeline of Ancient Egypt

This brief timeline of the history of ancient Egypt includes notes on historical characters that are either well known or are mentioned in the text. Dates are regnal dates unless otherwise noted.

Period	Dynasties	Dates
Archaic Period	1-2	c. 3000-2650 BCE

Hor-Aha (no definite dates)

Old Kingdom	3-8	c. 2650-2135 BCE

Djoser, second half of 26th century BCE (dates unclear)

Khafre, 2558-2532 BCE

Unas, 2375-2345 BCE

Teti, 2345-2323 BCE

Pepi I, 2321-2184 BCE

First Intermediate Period	9-11	c. 2135-2040 BCE
Middle Kingdom	11-14	c. 2040-1650 BCE

Amenemhet I, 1985-1955 BCE

Senusret I, 1965-1920 BCE

Senusret III, 1880-1855 BCE

Amenemhet III, 1855-1808 BCE

Hyksos Period/ Second Intermediate Period   15-17   c. 1650-1550 BCE

The Hyksos were foreign invaders, possibly from Western Asia

New Kingdom   18-20   c. 1550-1080 BCE

Ahmose I, 1550-1525 BCE

Thutmose II, 1492-1479 BCE

Hatshepsut, 1479-1458 BCE

Thutmose III, 1479-1425 BCE

Thutmose IV, 1479-1390 BCE

Amenhotep III, 1390-1352 BCE

Amenhotep IV / Akhenaten, "The Heretic King," 1353-1336 BCE

Tutankhamun, 1336-1327 BCE

Rameses II, r. 1279-1212 BCE

Late Period   21-31   c. 1080-332 BCE

The Late Period saw repeated incursions by outside rulers:

25th Dynasty (780-656 BCE): Cushite rulers

TAHARQA, 690-664 BCE

27th Dynasty (525-404 BCE): Persian rulers

28th-30th Dynasty (404-341 BCE): Egyptian pharaohs

Nectanebo II, 360–342 BCE

31ʳᵈ Dynasty (342–332 BCE): return of Persian rule

Alexander the Great (332–323 BCE)

Ptolemaic Period**323–30 BCE**

Rule by Macedonian Greeks after the death of Alexander

Ptolemy I Soter, 305–285 BCE

Cleopatra VII Philopator, 51–30 BCE

Roman Period**30 BCE–395 *CE***

Egypt annexed as part of the Roman Empire

Augustus, 31 BCE–14 CE

Tiberius, 14–37 CE

Caligula, 37–41 CE

Vespasian, 69–79 CE

Hadrian, 117–138 CE

Amen (Amun, Amon, Ammon)

Amen is an excellent example of the complexities of Egyptian religion, in the ways that religion changed across time, in how it was tied to local practice, and the ways in which it intersected with and was affected by politics in the Dynastic Period. Amen's two earliest manifestations were at Thebes and Hermopolis. In Thebes, Amen functioned as the main creator god of the city, having supplanted an earlier god named Montu, while in Hermopolis, he was one of the eight deities of the Ogdoad, a collection of four male and four female deities who created the universe and who were considered to be personifications of various important abstract concepts such as darkness or infinity. In Hermopolis, Amen, along with his consort Amaunet, was considered to be the personification of hiddenness, since his name literally means "hidden one" or "invisible." As such, he was associated with air and the wind.

There are several versions of the Hermopolitan creation myth, which is discussed in the chapter on the Ogdoad below. The Theban cosmogony makes use of the theme of the cosmic egg, which it has in common with some versions of the Hermopolitan myth. In the Theban myth, Amen hatches uncreated out of an egg that sits on the primeval mound; after this happens, he goes on to create the rest of the world. Thebes proudly asserted that the city was built on this primeval mound, thus asserting itself as the center of creation and the place of Amen's first emergence into being.

In Thebes, Amen became combined with the solar deity Ra, creating one all-powerful god called Amen-Ra. Other syncretizations of Amen joined him with Min, the god of fertility and virility, and with Ptah, another creator god whose main cult center was in Memphis. However, it was as Amen-Ra in the city of Thebes that Amen gained his greatest importance, both in terms of religious worship and in his connections to Egyptian political power.

Amen gained prestige and importance, and as Amen-Ra, he eventually became the principal god of Egypt during the New Kingdom. One reason for Amen's ascendancy from a secondary, local god of the city of Thebes to a national, all-powerful deity was the defeat of the Hyksos by Ahmose I. The Hyksos were immigrants to Egypt who gradually were able to seize considerable political power, especially in the southern part of the country, where Thebes is located. The period of Hyksos rule is known as the Second Intermediate Period. When Ahmose I defeated the Hyksos and drove them out of Egypt, he claimed that his victory was due to the favor of Amen, giving Amen a considerable boost in popularity and power, allowing Amen to supplant Montu, a war god who had been the main deity of Thebes up to that point.

As a national deity, Amen was said to be the husband of Mut, a sky goddess, and the father of Khonsu, the god of the moon. Together, these three deities were known as the Theban Triad, and they were worshiped at the massive temple complex at Karnak, one of the largest and most elaborate ancient Egyptian religious centers.

The newly syncretized god of Thebes, Amen-Ra, was given the role of father of the pharaoh, a shift from earlier times when the pharaoh was thought to be the son of Horus. Historian Samuel Kramer notes that, in this guise, Amen-Ra began to take on many of the characteristics now generally associated with the concept of God as elucidated in the Bible.[1] Like God, Amen-Ra was seen as an uncreated being who, through his own unlimited power, created the universe. Amen-Ra also subjugated the other gods under his power, was invisible and everywhere, and was able to manifest himself in various ways to humankind.

We see this concept of Amen-Ra as the all-powerful and one true god in a hymn written for Pinedjem II, the high priest of Amen-Ra from 990 to 969 BCE:

> This venerable god, Lord of all Gods, Amon-Re, Lord of the Throne(s) of the Two Lands, He who resides in He who Reckons the Thrones.
>
> Venerable manifestation which came into being in the beginning, Great God who lives on Truth, first Primeval One who engendered the primeval gods, out of whom all the other gods came into being.
>
> The Unique One, who created what exists at the first beginning of the earth. Mysterious of births, of numerous appearances, whose manifestations are not known.
>
> Venerable Power, beloved and feared, rich of appearances, Lord of Might, creative power, out of whose form came into being every form, he who came first into being, besides whom nothing exists.

---

[1] Samuel Noah Kramer, *Mythologies of the Ancient World* (Garden City: Doubleday, 1961), 47.

> He who gave light to the earth, for
> the first time with the disk. Light,
> Radiating One, when he appears, men
> live. When he sails the sky, he is not
> weary, early in the morning his work is
> already fixed.[2]

Although we can see how the character of Amen-Ra resonates with that of the biblical God in this hymn, we can also see some of the ways that Amen-Ra remains distinct. Amen-Ra may have been the supreme god of the Egyptians, but he was not the sole god, and his aspect as the god of the sun remains intact, as we see in the last verse, which refers specifically to the rising of the sun ("the disk") and its course across the sky during the day.

As the supreme god of Egypt, Amen-Ra was given pride of place through the construction of the great temple complex at Karnak. Although construction of the temple complex began in the Middle Kingdom during the reign of Senusret I, the bulk of it was built during the New Kingdom by Pharaoh Amenhotep III. The temple of Amen at Karnak is considered to be one of the largest religious structures in the world, and its hypostyle hall (an unroofed area made of multiple colossal pillars) and the giant, hieroglyphic-encrusted papyrus columns leading up to the entrance are images immediately recognizable to many people today.

This elevation of Amen-Ra to supreme god had political repercussions, both through the more widespread worship of Amen-Ra and through the symbol of his cult's visible temporal power at Karnak. Although many other temples to Amen-Ra were constructed at this time, the magnificence and sheer size of the Karnak temple gave it considerable status. The other factor in the cult's political

---

[2] Translation in Alexandre Piankoff, trans., and Natacha Rambova, ed., *Mythological Papyri: Texts* (New York: Pantheon Books, 1957), 18.

ascendency was the alliance of the priesthood of Amen-Ra with the monarchy.

This alliance began with the defeat of the Hyksos. As Samuel Kramer observes, when Ahmose I attributed his victory to Amen, he effectively shackled himself and his successors with a debt of gratitude that was expressed through the granting of land, treasure, and slaves to the priesthood of Amen as tangible signs of the king's thanks for Amen's protection.[3] As with so many endeavors that seem like a good idea at the time, the enrichment of the priesthood of Amen-Ra eventually proved disastrous for the pharaohs, because it siphoned power away from the monarchy and gave it to the priests. The Amen-Ra priesthood effectively became kingmakers because, as Kramer reports,

> the god's role as father of the king gave the priests considerable strength in selecting and supporting a particular candidate for the kingship.... Thus, by expressing or withholding divine approval, the priests of Amon-Re' [sic] could ensure their candidate was successful.[4]

Through their vast wealth and religious control over who might legitimately sit on the throne, the priesthood of Amen functioned in many ways as the *de facto* rulers of Egypt by the time of Amenhotep III.

However, it was not only the male heirs to the throne who claimed to be the children of Amen-Ra. When Queen Hatshepsut assumed the title of pharaoh upon the death of her husband, Thutmose II, she had an official myth created that claimed her birth to be ordained by none other than Amen-Ra himself. In the myth, Amen-Ra tells the assembled company of the gods that he wants to make a queen to rule over all of Egypt. He sends out Thoth to find a woman to be the

---

[3] Kramer, *Mythologies of the Ancient World*, 124.
[4] Kramer, *Mythologies of the Ancient World*, 124.

mother of this great queen, and when she is located, Amen-Ra impregnates her, and thus Hatshepsut is conceived. But Amen-Ra isn't done; he commissions the god Khnum, the ram-headed god of the Nile floods, to make Hatshepsut's body and soul on his potter's wheel. In this project, Khnum is helped by the goddess Hekt, a fertility goddess also associated with the flooding of the Nile. Thus, not only was Hatshepsut the daughter of Amen-Ra, but her very body and soul were created by the gods at Amen-Ra's command.

Hatshepsut needed this myth in order to promote the legitimacy of her rule, because she originally took the throne not as the direct heir of the pharaoh but rather as the dowager queen regent to her infant son, who later became Thutmose III. In Hatshepsut, we see how a ruler might manipulate the power of Amen-Ra's cult in order to further her own political ambitions, which stands in stark distinction to the situation under later pharaohs, who essentially were under the thumbs of Amen-Ra's priests.

Alexander the Great was another ruler who seized upon the popularity of Amen-Ra in order to legitimize his own rule. When Alexander conquered Egypt in 331 BCE, he claimed that he was the son of Ammon-Zeus, a syncretization of the Greek supreme god Zeus with the Egyptian Amen. Amen was also adopted by the Romans as Ammon-Jupiter.

The primary challenge to the power of Amen-Ra and his priests came during the rule of Amenhotep IV. Sometimes known as the "heretic king," Amenhotep changed his name to Akhenaten in the fifth year of his reign and began a series of sweeping religious reforms intended to shift all worship to a single solar deity, Aten. Akhenaten's reforms are discussed in detail in the chapter on Aten below.

The national worship of Amen was weakened somewhat because of Akhenaten's reforms, and it further waned during the tenth century BCE, although his cult remained important in Thebes. Amen was eclipsed particularly during the Ptolemaic Period, when Isis and Serapis became a central focus of worship not only in Egypt but also in many communities in Greece and Rome. Amen's cult was not erased entirely until Christianity was established as a state religion in the mid-fifth century CE.

Anubis (Anpu, Inpw)

With his black jackal's head perched upon a man's body, Anubis is one of the most easily identified ancient Egyptian deities. Some depictions of this god show him holding the ankh, or symbol of life, in one hand and a staff in the other, while other images show him tending to the dead body of a pharaoh. This association with death and decay is one of Anubis's chief characteristics. Indeed, his name in Egyptian, *Anpu*, literally means "decay" ("Anubis" is the Greek form of the name), and it is possible that the use of the jackal's head as one of the attributes of this god may be a reference to the tendency of jackals to scavenge in cemeteries and other places where dead bodies are found.

Although Anubis was always considered to be a god of death and the dead, his position within Egyptian religion altered over time. During the First Dynasty, Anubis was the primary god of the dead, but this changed during the Middle Kingdom, when the cult of Osiris gained popularity and Osiris was elevated to the supreme god of the dead and lord of the Tuat, the ancient Egyptian Underworld. Anubis may have lost his throne to Osiris, but he did not lose his importance; instead, his role shifted from ruler of the dead to embalmer and judge.

The myths surrounding Anubis's origins and parentage also changed over time. In some early myths, Anubis is said to be the son of the sun god Ra and the brother of Osiris, Isis, Nephthys, and Set, either by the sky goddess Nut or the cow-headed goddess Hesat. In later myths, he is considered to be the son of Nephthys, who tricked Osiris into having intercourse with her. This shift likely had to do with the increasing importance of the Osiris cult and the need to incorporate Anubis into a new mythical and religious framework that centered on Osiris, rather than Anubis, as the god of the dead.

One of Anubis's chief duties in the Tuat was the judging of souls to see whether or not they were worthy of eternal life. When the soul of a deceased person came before Anubis, Anubis weighed their heart against the feather of truth. The deceased person then had to vow that they had lived a good life full of good deeds. If the person was telling the truth, the heart would weigh less than the feather, and the person would be allowed into the delights of the afterlife. If the person was lying, however, the heart would weigh more than the feather, and the person would be condemned to obliteration by being devoured by Ammit, a goddess with the head of a crocodile, the forequarters of a lion, and the hindquarters of a hippopotamus.

Anubis was also the god of embalming, a role that became important after the rise of the Osiris cult. When Isis finds Osiris's dead body, Anubis helps her embalm it and wrap it in linen wrappings. The other part of the embalming process was the preservation of the stomach, intestines, lungs, and liver, which were placed into jars made of earthenware, alabaster, or other hard, non-porous materials. These jars sometimes had stoppers carved or molded into the likeness of gods who had the responsibility for looking after these organs, which the deceased person was believed to get back after death. This tradition of preserving the organs also comes from the Osiris myth, since Anubis was given Osiris's organs after Osiris died.

As with several other gods in the Egyptian pantheon, Anubis became absorbed into Greco-Roman religious practices during the Ptolemaic Period. Anubis was often syncretized with the Greek god Hermes, who had the task of conducting souls to Hades. In this way, Anubis gained a function as a guide of souls in addition to his other duties as embalmer, judge of the dead, and protector of tombs and cemeteries.

Ancient Egyptian writings that mention Anubis include the Pyramid Texts, which are inscriptions inside a series of Old Kingdom pyramids that were built for five pharaohs and some of their wives. These texts, which preserve spells and prayers intended to raise the occupant of the tomb from the dead and guide them to eternal life, place Anubis in various roles with respect to the deceased. Some of the spells suggest that the dead person would themselves become Anubis in some way, while others refer to the god's duties as embalmer and the guide and transformer of souls. Below are some examples from the tomb of Pharaoh Pepi I:

> Awake for Horus, stand up against Seth! Raise yourself as Osiris, as the akh [soul] who is Geb's first son, and take up your position as Anubis on the shrine.[5]

> So, [Pepi] will go forth to the sky, his wingtips those of a big bird. His entrails have been washed by Anubis, and Horus's service in Abydos—Osiris's purification—has been performed.[6]

---

[5] James P. Allen, *The Ancient Egyptian Pyramid Texts* (Atlanta: Society of Biblical Literature), 105.

[6] Allen, *Pyramid Texts*, 158. Abydos refers to the ancient Egyptian city by that name, where a royal necropolis was located. Bracketed insert is mine.

> Anubis, foremost of the god's booth, has commanded that you descend as a star, as the morning god.[7]
>
> Your akh is about [you, father Osiris Pepi], as a king-given offering that shall exist for you as one that Anubis made for you.[8]

In these texts, it is Anubis himself who embalms the pharaoh and who transforms him into a divine being, a process that includes the pharaoh taking on the identity of Anubis for himself. The last section of the text also suggests that the soul of the pharaoh—likely in its resurrected state—is something created specifically for the pharaoh by Anubis.

Anubis had a presence and a function outside of funerary texts and royal burials, however. "The Tale of Two Brothers," an Egyptian folktale from the New Kingdom, tells the story of Anubis and Bata, brothers who initially live in the same household together, along with Anubis's wife. In this story, Bata acts as a herdsman and worker on Anubis's land. All goes well until Anubis's wife tries to seduce Bata. When Bata refuses her advances, she pretends that he has assaulted her. Anubis initially believes his wife's story, and Bata barely escapes with his life. As part of his oath to Anubis that he is telling the truth, Bata cuts off his penis and throws it into the river. He then runs into the wilderness, where he builds a house for himself. He places his heart at the top of an acacia tree that grows nearby.

The gods see that Bata is living alone and so provide a wife for him. Bata tells her not to leave the house, because the sea desires her and will snatch her away. When the wife disobeys Bata, the sea tries to abduct her, but the woman runs too fast and manages to get safely back into the house. As the woman is running away, the sea tells the

---

[7] Allen, *Pyramid Texts*, 168.
[8] Allen, *Pyramid Texts*, 195. Bracketed insert in the original.

acacia tree to grab her, but the tree only manages to get a lock of her hair, which falls into the water.

The hair floats down the river to the place where the pharaoh's launderers are doing the wash. The pharaoh's clothing picks up the scent of Bata's wife's perfume, and the pharaoh commands the woman to be brought to him. When she arrives, she becomes the pharaoh's wife, and she soon tells the pharaoh about the acacia tree that holds Bata's heart. The pharaoh commands that the tree be destroyed. Cutting down the tree kills Bata.

Anubis is alerted to Bata's death by certain signs. Anubis then goes looking for his brother and finds Bata's dead body on the bed inside his house. Bata had told Anubis that his heart was to be stored outside of his body, so Anubis goes looking for it. After a long search, he finds the heart and restores it to Bata's body, which brings Bata back to life. Bata then transforms himself into a magical bull and tells Anubis to ride him to the court of the pharaoh.

Bata's former wife, who is still living at the royal court as the wife of the pharaoh, learns that her husband has transformed himself into a bull and means to get revenge on her, so she arranges for the bull to be sacrificed and cut into pieces. However, her plans are foiled when two drops of the bull's blood land outside the doors of the temple. From this blood, two trees sprout up, one of which accuses the woman of treachery as she sits in its shade.

Bata's former wife arranges for the trees to be cut down and chopped up, but a splinter from the tree that spoke to her goes into her mouth and impregnates her. For a second time, Bata is brought back from the dead, for the infant borne by Bata's former wife is Bata himself, who goes on to become pharaoh. The story ends with Bata pronouncing judgment on his former wife and making Anubis his heir.

Although Bata was a New Kingdom god in his own right, it is easy to see the parallels between his story and the myth of the dying and rising Osiris, as well as between the role of Anubis in this story and his functions elsewhere in Egyptian myth. Bata clearly plays the role of Osiris; his severed penis ends up in a river, and he is brought back to life after having died through the ministrations of Anubis. Like Osiris, Bata becomes imprisoned in the wood of a tree, and he later is restored to full life a second time, after which he comes into his power as the lord of the land.

Just as the adventures of Bata represent the journey of Osiris from life to death to resurrection to kingship, so, too, does Anubis maintain his traditional funerary role in this tale. It is Anubis's duty to find and tend to the body of the dead Bata and to restore him to life through his magic by placing Bata's heart back in his body. This parallels Anubis's work in helping to embalm the dead Osiris, thus restoring him to life. Anubis also acts as a sort of guide for Bata when Bata takes on the form of a bull, and when Bata enters into his authority as pharaoh, Anubis is given an important role as the crown prince of the realm, just as Anubis was given important authority in the Tuat under the kingship of Osiris.

Anubis's association with death and judgment, as well as the imposing image of his black jackal's head and muscular body, often lead modern people to see him as a fearsome and potentially violent god. However, as we have seen, ancient Egyptian people did not view Anubis that way. For the ancient Egyptians, Anubis was a god who tenderly cared for the dead and whose gifts and power allowed the souls of the just to enter eternal life.

Aten (Aton)

The god Aten was identified with the sun disk and was considered to be a creator god who made all things and who sustained the universe by his power. Because the Egyptian word "aten" means "disk," this god is sometimes referred to as "the Aten," or "the sun disk." The earliest depictions of the Aten show it as a man with a falcon's head, but eventually the Aten came to be depicted as the sun giving off many rays or as a disk with outstretched wings. These depictions reflect the understanding of Aten as a god of light who is everywhere, who cannot be defined by a particular form, and whose *ba*, or spiritual essence, cannot be represented by an earthly animal.

Worship of Aten is most commonly associated with the reign of Pharaoh Amenhotep IV, who took the name Akhenaten and who attempted to elevate the Aten cult above all others. However, worship of the sun disk as an all-powerful god actually began before Akhenaten took the throne. As Egyptologist George Hart states, "The worship of Aten was not a sudden innovation on the part of one king, but the climax of a religious quest among Egyptians for a benign god limitless in power and manifest in all countries and all natural phenomena."[9]

---

[9] George Hart, *A Dictionary of Egyptian Gods and Goddesses* (London:

Akhenaten's royal transference of the worship of Amen-Ra to the worship of Aten, not only as the primary deity but as the sole god of Egypt, had some of its roots in religious and political changes that had taken place hundreds of years earlier, with Ahmose I's defeat of the Hyksos and the elevation of the cult of Amen-Ra, which in turn greatly increased the power of Amen-Ra's priests. Declaring a different god to be both supreme and the primary patron of the pharaoh had the effect of gutting the authority of Amen-Ra's priesthood and restoring to the pharaohs some of their lost power.

The earliest mention of the Aten as a divine concept, if not a separate deity in its own right, extends back to the Middle Kingdom. We find this in an ancient Egyptian tale known as "The Story of Sinuhe," a first-person narrative purportedly written by a highly placed official at the court of the pharaoh. Early in the narrative, Sinuhe announces the death of the Twelfth Dynasty pharaoh Amenemhet I, who died in 1955 BCE. Sinuhe says, "He [the pharaoh] penetrated the sky, being joined to the sun disk [the Aten], the God's body being mixed with that of him who made him."[10]

Increasing reverence for the Aten as a separate divine being, rather than as a divine concept or avatar of the sun god Ra, is a phenomenon of the early New Kingdom. Thutmose IV evidently saw the Aten as a god in its own right, since "[d]uring his rule an historical text on the underside of a scarab mentions Aten in the vanguard of the pharaoh's army in battle—a role commonly given to Amun."[11] Thutmose's successor, Amenhotep III (Akhenaten's father), seems to have had a personal devotion to the Aten, although he did not neglect the more traditional worship of Amen-Ra. Apparently, Amenhotep III saw no contradictions between his devotion to Amen-Ra and his worship of

---

Routledge, 2000), 37.

[10] William Kelly Simpson, ed., *The Literature of Ancient Egypt: An Anthology of Stories, Instructions, Stelae, Autobiographies, and Poetry* (New Haven: Yale University Press, 2003), 55. Bracketed insertions are mine.

[11] Hart, *Dictionary*, 38.

Aten, since evidence of his reverence for the former includes construction on the great temple of Amen-Ra at Karnak. Evidence of his devotion to the latter includes authorizing construction of a temple to the Aten in Heliopolis (literally "City of the Sun"), taking the name Tekhen-Aten ("Radiance of Aten") as one of his many epithets, and naming his royal barge *Aten-Tjehen* ("Shining Sun Disk").

It was left to Amenhotep III's son Amenhotep IV (later Akhenaten) to take the next steps in the development of the Aten cult. This project began in the fifth year of Amenhotep IV's reign. One of his first steps was to change his name from one meaning "Amen is Pleased" to one meaning "Useful to Aten." That move was highly significant in itself, because it took away the focus on reverence for Amen-Ra as the supreme state god and progenitor of the pharaohs and instead allied the throne with a relatively new deity whose status paled in comparison to that of Amen-Ra, in both political and religious terms.

One of Akhenaten's actions in elevating the cult of the Aten was to move the royal residence from Thebes to a new city called Akhetaten, which means "Horizon of the Aten." Construction of the city began in the fifth year of Akhenaten's reign and was completed a few years later. Akhetaten was located in central Egypt in what is now Amarna, standing about halfway between the ancient city of Thebes to the south and Memphis to the north at the mouth of the Nile Delta. Akhetaten boasted two new temples to the Aten, one small and one large and grand, as well as living quarters for the pharaoh, his family, and his court. Housing was also provided for various nobles, who thought it wise and status-raising to live close to the pharaoh, and for the various administrators and functionaries of both the Egyptian state and the sacred temples to Aten.

Worship of the Aten took place every day. Akhenaten officiated as high priest, although there were other, lesser priests also dedicated to the service of the Aten. On some occasions, Queen Nefertiti and other royal women participated in worship services. Temples to the

Aten were different from those dedicated to other gods in that the Aten's temples had no roofs, in order that the light of the sun might shine into the sanctuary.

By Akhenaten's time, the representation of Aten as having a mixed human-animal form had long been abandoned in favor of a depiction of the sun and its rays, a representation that is, in some ways, more abstract than depictions of other Egyptian deities, since it avoids anthropomorphization in favor of an image of solar—and, hence, divine—power. We see this in one important relief from the Great Temple in Akhetaten, which shows Akhenaten, Nefertiti, and their daughter Meritaten holding up fronds of papyrus while offering worship to the Aten, which is depicted as a disk from which rays pour down onto the pharaoh, his wife, and his child. Some of the rays end in human hands that are poised in a gesture of benediction, while other hands hold ankhs, the Egyptian symbol of life, signifying the lifegiving power of the Aten.

When Akhenaten built his new city and new temples, he intended them to usher in a new era in which the Aten was not only the supreme god but also the only god, who was revered both in itself and in its manifestation in the person of the king. Worship of Amen-Ra was forbidden, as was devotion to Osiris. Temples to the old gods were closed, and their wealth and income were devoted instead to the worship of the Aten. Because of this, Akhenaten is sometimes considered to be an early monotheist, but scholarly opinion is divided over the degree to which Atenism was, in fact, a monotheistic faith.

In addition to building temples and commissioning artworks that showed Akhenaten venerating the Aten, Akhenaten also wrote a hymn to the sun. Hymns to the gods had always been an important part of Egyptian religious practice, so the writing of a hymn was nothing new in itself. What was new, however, is the way that Akhenaten describes the Aten and the believer's relationship to it. Some scholars have compared Akhenaten's hymn to Psalm 104, which similarly praises the God of the Israelites and lists his creative acts. Below are some excerpts from Akhenaten's hymn, side by side with the relevant passages of Psalm 104 from the New International Version:

Akhenaten's Hymn[12]

You rise in perfection on the horizon of the sky,

living Aten, who determines life.

Whenever you are risen upon the eastern horizon

you fill every land with your perfection.

You are appealing, great, sparkling, high over every land;

your rays embrace the lands as far as everything you have made.

. . . .

Whenever you set on the western horizon,

the land is in darkness in the manner of death.

They sleep in a bedroom with heads under the covers,

Psalm 104

The Lord wraps himself in light as with a garment;

he stretches out the heavens like a tent

and lays the beams of his upper chambers on their waters.

He makes the clouds his chariot

and rides on the wings of the wind.

He makes winds his messengers,

flames of fire his servants. (vv. 2-4)

He made the moon to mark the seasons,

and the sun knows when to go down.

You bring darkness, it becomes night,

---

[12] Kelly, *Literature of Ancient Egypt*, 279-80, 283.

and one eye cannot see another.

. . . .

Every lion comes out of his cave and all the serpents bite,

for darkness is a blanket.

The land is silent now, because He who makes them

is at rest on His horizon.

. . . .

and all the beasts of the forest prowl.

The lions roar for their prey

and seek their food from God. (vv. 19-21)

The entire land performs its work:

all the flocks are content with their fodder,

trees and plants grow,

birds fly up to their nests,

their wings extended in praise for your *Ka*.

All the kine prance on their feet;

everything which flies up and alights,

they live when you rise for them.

The barges sail upstream and downstream too,

for every way is open at your rising.

The fishes in the river leap before your face

How many are your works, Lord!

In wisdom you made them all;

the earth is full of your creatures.

There is the sea, vast and spacious,

teeming with creatures beyond number—

living things both large and small.

There the ships go to and fro,

and Leviathan, which you formed to frolic there.

when your rays are inside the sea.
....

The earth comes forth into existence by your hand,
and you make it.
When you rise, they live;
when you set, they die.
....

All creatures look to you to give them their food at the proper time. (vv. 24–27)

When you give it to them, they gather it up;
when you open your hand,
they are satisfied with good things.
When you hide your face, they are terrified;
when you take away their breath,
they die and return to the dust. (vv. 28–29)

Akhenaten's fervent personal devotion to the Aten was not sufficient to bring about the religious revolution he so desired. Atenism failed to make much headway among the Egyptian populace, who resented the loss of their traditional religion and who were grateful when Akhenaten's heir, Tutankhamen, revived the worship of Amen-Ra, Osiris, and the other gods who had been revered by Egyptians for millennia. During this restoration, the old temples were reopened and the priesthoods restored, and the city of Akhetaten was destroyed by royal command. Akhenaten was treated as a heretic, and his name erased from inscriptions.

Modern opinions of Akhenaten are highly variable. Some authors and scholars have seen him in much the same way as his countrymen apparently did, as a heretic whose religious fervor bordered on mania. Others, however, have seen him as a sincere reformer who wished to replace a polytheistic system with one devoted to a single supreme deity. Those who espouse the latter opinion sometimes try to align Akhenaten's faith with Christianity, attempting to show that Akhenaten was ahead of his time and that his reforms were an improvement. However, most scholars today agree that comparisons of Atenism with other monotheistic religions need to be done carefully in order to avoid both the creation of false parallels between Atenism and other religions and also to steer clear of the assumption that monotheism is somehow superior to other religious expressions.

In addition to receiving significant scholarly attention, Pharaoh Akhenaten has also captured the imagination of modern artists and musicians. One important artwork is the opera *Akhnaten* by the American minimalist composer Philip Glass. *Akhnaten* was written in 1983, and draws its libretto partly from ancient Egyptian texts and partly from a set of letters in Akkadian that were found in the ruins of Akhetaten. Other portions of the libretto are in biblical Hebrew. Each performance of the opera includes a setting of Akhenaten's "Hymn to the Sun," which is always sung in the language of the audience that is watching at the time. The action of the opera starts with the funeral of his father, Amenhotep III. The opera then follows the course of Akhenaten's life, from his coronation to his own death and burial.

The 2016 production by the English National Opera, which was revived in 2018 and 2019, included the Gandini juggling troupe. The troupe's juggling of balls and clubs of various sizes was intended to be symbolic of some of the themes of the opera, and was timed to mesh with and represent the flow of the music.

Atum (Tum, Tem, Atem, Temu)

One of the primary creator gods of ancient Egypt, Atum was said to have emerged on the primeval mound that sat in the primeval waters, which were personified as the god Nun. Atum's name means something like "all" or "complete." His first act of creation was to make Shu, the god of air, and Tefnut, the goddess of light. One version of the story says that Atum made them from his semen, while another says that Shu was made from Atum's spittle and that he vomited Tefnut into existence. From Shu and Tefnut came Geb, the god of the earth, and Nut, the goddess of the sky. Geb and Nut's children were Isis, Osiris, Nephthys, and Set. Together, Atum and his descendants are referred to as the Ennead, the primary deities worshiped in Heliopolis, an ancient city near what is now Cairo. Egyptologist Stephen Quirke notes that before the New Kingdom, Atum and the Ennead were more widely considered to be the primary creator deities throughout Egypt.[13]

Like many other gods, Atum quickly became identified with the sun god Ra, and he was frequently worshiped as Atum-Ra. However, Atum also had his own independent role with respect to solar

---

[13] Stephen Quirke, *Exploring Religion in Ancient Egypt* (Chichester: John Wiley & Sons, 2015), 137.

theology. Ancient Egyptians personified the sun as different deities depending on the time of day. In this system, Atum was the setting sun, while Ra was the sun at midday and Khepera was the rising sun.

The connection between Atum and light is clearly drawn in the myth of the Eye of Ra and the creation of human beings. In this myth, Shu and Tefnut become separated from Atum in the vastness of Nun, so Atum sends his Eye to look for them. While the Eye is away, Atum grows a new one. When the first Eye returns triumphantly with Shu and Tefnut, Atum weeps for joy, and from his tears human beings are created. The first Eye becomes jealous of the second one, so Atum gives the first one pride of place by turning it into the sun disk and putting it on his head.

In addition to his roles as creator and an aspect of the sun, Atum was thought to sometimes take on the form of an ichneumon (Egyptian mongoose). Author Margaret R. Bunson states that this was because of the mongoose's ability to kill venomous serpents without taking harm and because it ate crocodile eggs.[14]

---

[14] Margaret R. Bunson, *Encyclopedia of Ancient Egypt*, rev. ed. (New York: Facts on File, Inc., 2002), 177.

Bastet (Bast, Boubastis, Pasht)

Goddess of fertility and motherhood, protector of the pharaoh, and identified with the Eye of Ra, the cat-headed goddess Bastet originally was conceptualized as a lion-headed deity and often was aligned with Sekhmet, another lion-headed goddess. In fact, Bastet and Sekhmet sometimes were treated as two different facets of the same deity. Because of Bastet's association with Sekhmet, she was also linked with the cow-headed goddess Hathor, who transformed into Sekhmet and destroyed humanity at the command of Ra.

In her cat-headed form, Bastet (also known as Bast) is usually portrayed as having a woman's body, clothed in a linen sheath dress, and carrying a sistrum (a type of rattle) and a box or jar. Both the actual meaning and pronunciation of Bastet's name remain unclear. Egyptologist Geraldine Pinch has suggested that it means something like "She of the Ointment Jar," because Bastet was associated with ointments and perfumes.[15]

Bastet was venerated in her lion form for the first thousand years of Egyptian dynastic history. The shift to her cat form occurred sometime during the second millennium BCE. Pinch notes that the

---

[15] Geraldine Pinch, *A Handbook of Egyptian Mythology* (Santa Barbara: ABC-CLIO, 2002), 115.

different aspects of Bastet "as nurturing mother and terrifying avenger" can be found in many different sources. These include the Pyramid Texts, which date from c. 2400 to 2300 BCE ; the Coffin Texts, which are protective spells written on the insides of coffins, dating from c. 2181 to 2185 BCE; and in the *Book of the Dead*, a New Kingdom funerary text that contains collections of spells and prayers intended to shepherd the soul through the hazards of the Underworld.[16]

Ideas about Bastet's character, as depicted in the myths that involve her, revolved in part around the observed behavior of cats. Bastet was associated with fertility and motherhood because cats themselves are both very fertile and also devoted, attentive mothers. The ferocity of the cat, on the other hand, is shown in a myth in which Bastet helps Ra kill the serpent-demon Apep (also known as Apophis) by attacking it with her claws. The cat's independence and unwillingness to be tamed is reflected in a myth usually referred to as "The Distant Goddess," in which Bastet, in her guise as the Eye of Ra and in feline form, runs away into the desert, and Ra has to send a god (which one varies depending on the version of the story) to coax her to come back home. Geraldine Pinch notes that in Ptolemaic Egypt, the return of the Distant Goddess had importance to the Egyptian calendar and to beliefs about the origin of the Nile floods, since the goddess's return home was said to initiate the inundation of the Nile, which was seen as the beginning of the Egyptian year.[17]

The worship of Bastet was centered in the city of Bubastis, located on the eastern edge of the Nile Delta, where the goddess had a fine temple. The worship of Bastet included votive offerings of bronze cat statuettes and actual mummified cats. The ancient historian Herodotus, who refers to Bastet as the Roman goddess Diana,

---

[16] Pinch, *Handbook*, 115.
[17] Pinch, *Handbook*, 90.

thought the Temple of Bastet the most beautiful in Egypt.[18] In his description of the temple precincts, Herodotus says that two canals ran from the Nile to the entrance, "one flowing round it on one side, the other on the other," and that trees had been planted along the edges of each canal.[19] In addition, Herodotus says that the temple grounds were surrounded by a wall "sculptured with figures ... and within is a grove of lofty trees, planted round a large temple."[20]

Herodotus also wrote a description of the main festival of Bastet, which historian Lewis Spence says was held in April and May every year.[21] Bastet's festival appears to have been one of the most popular feasts in the Egyptian calendar, drawing up to 700,000 visitors to Bubastis every year, according to Herodotus.[22] This festival was an occasion for great rejoicing, celebrated with sacrifices, processions of barges down the river, music, singing and dancing, and the consumption of enormous amounts of alcohol. Indeed, Herodotus estimated that at the festival of Bastet, "more wine is consumed ... than in all the rest of the year."[23] It is possible that the volume of wine consumed at Bastet's festival was related to the myth of Hathor/Sekhmet, in which the goddess's bloodlust is sated by beer brewed by Ra, which has been colored to look like blood so that Hathor/Sekhmet would drink that rather than the blood of the people. The ruse works; Hathor/Sekhmet drinks until she is senseless, and after that point she has no more desire to kill.

---

[18] Herodotus II:137; Henry Cary, trans., *Herodotus* (London: George Bell and Sons, 1901), 150.

[19] Herodotus II:137; Cary, trans., 150.

[20] Herodotus II:137; Cary, trans. 150.

[21] Lewis Spence, *Myths and Legends of Ancient Egypt* (Boston: David D. Nickerson & Co., [1915]), 148.

[22] Herodotus II:60; Cary, trans., 118.

[23] Herodotus II:60; Cary, trans., 118.

The Book of the Dead and Other Funerary Texts

Since the Old Kingdom, it had been an Egyptian funerary tradition to write prayers and spells on the walls of the tombs of the pharaohs, to give them the information and power they needed to navigate the dangers of the Tuat and attain eternal life. In the Middle Kingdom, such texts were written inside the coffins of the aristocracy, but during the New Kingdom, collections of prayers and spells began to be produced for any Egyptian person who might have the money to purchase them. These collections, which were written on papyrus scrolls and often illustrated, are referred to as the *Book of the Dead*. The various versions of the *Book of the Dead* constitute some of the most important sources of information about Egyptian myth, cosmology, religion, and funerary practices.

Although these collections are given a single, unitary title, they are far from uniform. Some collections are considerably longer and more lavishly illustrated than others, and it was possible for the person buying one of these books to have them custom-made by selecting which spells and prayers might be included. Other versions of the book seem to have been mass-produced, although the name of the person who bought them could be written inside at the time of purchase.

The *Book of the Dead* was intended to be buried with the deceased so that they could use it to deal with any dangers they might encounter when they arrived in the Tuat. One particularly important section of this book dealt with what one must do during the ceremony of the weighing of the heart, which would determine whether the deceased would be allowed to go on to paradise or whether they would be annihilated forever.

Another funerary text that came into regular use during the New Kingdom was the *Book of the Gates*. The *Book of the Gates* described the twelve sectors of the Underworld and the journey of the sun from west to east during the night, which made it similar to the *Amduat*, another important text. (The *Amduat* is summarized in the chapter on the Tuat below.) The sections of the *Book of the Gates* are aligned with the twelve hours of the night, and each one is populated by different collections of deities and other beings who attempt to either help or hinder Ra on his passage through their territories, a structure shared with the *Amduat*.

Each region of the Tuat in the *Book of the Gates* is described as having a specific gate with its own specific name, and each gate is guarded by a different serpent. For example, the gate of the third hour is named "Mistress of Nurturing," and the guardian serpent is called "the Stinger," while the gate of the seventh hour is called "Gleaming One," and its guardian serpent is called "Hidden Eye."[24]

While the *Book of the Dead* provided protection to the deceased and the *Book of the Gates* explained what the Tuat was like, the *Book of the Opening of the Mouth* contained detailed instructions for the Rite of the Opening of the Mouth, an important funerary liturgy that was performed both on statues and on the mummified remains of

---

[24] Pat Remler, *Egyptian Mythology A to Z*, 3rd ed. (New York: Chelsea House, 2010), 30-31.

deceased persons. Because Egyptian funerary beliefs and practices included offerings of food and drink to the deceased, the Rite of the Opening of the Mouth was vital for allowing the dead person to be able to consume the offerings in the afterlife. Egyptologist Ann Macy Roth has argued that the procedure used in this ritual was intended to mimic

> the birth and maturation of a child. Its purpose was to take the newly reborn deceased person through the transitions of birth and childhood, so that he or she could be nourished by the (adult) food provided in such profusion by Egyptian mortuary cults. The ritual therefore emphasized the aspects of the process that affected the way a child receives nourishment: the initial connection with the placenta, the severing of the umbilical cord, nursing, weaning, and teething.[25]

The rite could have up to seventy-five sections, but less elaborate versions were also performed. Special tools and objects used in the ceremony included incense, ointment, and water, which were all used to purify the statue, and clothing in which the statue was dressed. One particularly important implement was an adze or chisel that was used to ritually "open" the mouth of the statue or the deceased person so that they could breathe, eat, and drink. The *Book of the Dead* refers to this aspect of the ceremony in Chapter 23:

> My mouth is opened by Ptah,
>
> My mouth's bonds are loosed by my city-god.
>
> Thoth has come fully equipped with spells,
>
> He looses the bonds of Seth from my mouth.
>
> Atum has given me my hands,

---

[25] Ann Macy Roth, "Fingers, Stars, and the 'Opening of the Mouth': The Nature and Function of the *nṯrwj*-Blades," *The Journal of Egyptian Archaeology* 79 (1993): 60.

>They are placed as guardians.
>
>My mouth is given to me,
>
>My mouth is opened by Ptah
>
>With that chisel of metal
>
>With which he opened the mouth of the gods.[26]

As with other funerary texts, the *Book of the Opening of the Mouth* contains both illustrations and text. However, in the *Book of the Opening of the Mouth*, the illustrations have a different function than those in the *Amduat*, for example. Rather than descriptions of a particular space or collection of deities, the illustrations in the *Book of the Opening of the Mouth* accompany the text explaining how each part of the rite was to be performed. The pictures show who ought to be doing what, as well as how various items such as water were to be utilized.[27]

One interesting aspect of the performance of the Rite of the Opening of the Mouth was the continuum it created between the mortal world and the divine one. Living human priests and their helpers performed the rite on statues and on the mummified bodies of deceased people, but so did funerary gods such as Anubis and Wepwawet, who are sometimes depicted as engaged in actions from the rite. Further, some of the human actors in the rite performed by living priests might take on the role of deities. For example, in the version of the rite preserved in the tomb of pharaoh Seti I, two women participated in the story by representing the goddesses Isis and Nephthys.[28] These human stand-ins for deities, on the one hand, and the pictures of deities performing human actions, on the other,

---

[26] Miriam Lichtheim, *Ancient Egyptian Literature: A Book of Readings*, Vol. 2: *The New Kingdom* (Berkeley: University of California Press, 1976), 120.

[27] A complete edition of the book as it exists in the tomb of Seti I is E. A. Wallace Budge, *The Book of Opening the Mouth: The Egyptian Texts With English Translations* (London: Kegan Paul, Trench, Trübner & Co., Ltd., 1909), 2 vols.

[28] Budge, *Opening the Mouth* I, 12.

created a complex of links and alignments among myths, religious beliefs, and funerary practices that connected the divine and human worlds, as well as connecting the living and the dead. This is so because the deceased was often thought to become Osiris after death, so as to enter into everlasting life, and since Osiris was mourned by Isis and Nephthys after he was murdered by Set, so too did the deceased person require someone to represent these goddesses so that they might be properly mourned just as Osiris was.

The Four Sons of Horus

The sons of Horus the Elder had several roles within Egyptian religious and cosmological belief. In terms of cosmology, they were thought to be the four pillars that held up the sky, and they were often associated with the four cardinal directions. However, the greater part of their function was in relation to funerary practices, since they were thought to assist the transit of the soul into the afterlife. They are often depicted in funerary papyri, and in the Pyramid Texts, they are called upon to protect and guide the soul of the pharaoh as it enters the afterlife. Sculpted heads of the sons of Horus sometimes were used as guardians of the canopic jars used in mummification.

Ancient Egyptian burial practices involved the careful removal of the internal organs preparatory to embalming the body. The stomach, intestines, lungs, and liver were each placed in their own special jars, sometimes known as "canopic jars." These organs were carefully preserved and buried with the rest of the body, since the ancient Egyptians believed that the organs would be reunited with the body in the afterlife. (The heart was left inside the body so that it could be used in the ceremony of the weighing of the heart.)

The style of the lids for the canopic jars underwent changes as time passed. The oldest jars have plain lids, while those from the First

Intermediate Period are decorated with human heads. During the New Kingdom, the style changed yet again, with each lid being fashioned to represent one of the four sons of Horus the Elder. Each of these gods was associated with a specific protector goddess, and each had a specific role as a guardian of one of the preserved organs.

Duamutef

Duamutef had the head of a jackal. He was the guardian of the stomach, and was associated with the east. His guardian goddess was Neith.

Hapy (1; also Hapi)

Hapy had the head of a baboon and protected the lungs. He was associated with the north, and his guardian goddess was Nephthys. (For the deity of the same name who was associated with the Nile floods, see Hapy (2) below).

Imsety (Imset, Imseti, Amset, Amsety, Mesti, Mesta)

Associated with the south, Imsety had human form and protected the liver. His guardian goddess was Isis.

Qebehsenuef (Qebhsenuf)

Qebehsenuef's guardian was Serket, a goddess of fertility and healing, who was especially associated with protection against venomous stings and bites. Qebehsenuef was depicted as having a hawk's head. He was associated with the east and protected the intestines.

Geb (Seb, Keb, Kebb, Gebb)

The offspring of Shu and Tefnut, Geb was the god of earth, and his consort was the sky goddess Nut. Geb was part of the Ennead (Nine Gods) of the city of Heliopolis, a group of deities that included Geb's father, wife, and children. In visual representations, Geb is often depicted together with Shu and Nut. In these images, Geb lies on the ground, while Nut arches her body over him, with only her fingers and toes touching him at the ends of his body. Meanwhile, Shu stands in the middle of Geb's body, where he holds Nut up with his arms. This represents the sky arching over the earth, with air both separating the earth from the sky and also keeping the sky in position.

Like Osiris, Geb was sometimes depicted in myth as a pseudo-historical king of Egypt. However, unlike Osiris, who is a just and gentle god, Geb is ruthless, jealous, and violent. In a myth from the Thirtieth Dynasty that is preserved in a shrine in Phakussa (now Faqus) on the eastern edge of the Nile Delta, Geb's father Shu holds the throne of Egypt, and has ruled for a very long time. Geb is jealous of his father's power and is still angry that Shu separated him from his beloved wife, Nut. Geb leads a revolt that ousts Shu, after which Geb rapes his mother, Tefnut. Nine days of howling winds and violent storms follow Geb's actions, but when everything dies down, Geb takes the throne and is acknowledged as the king. When Geb attempts to take his father's crown, the *uraeus*, or cobra, that adorns it spits out venom that burns Geb and kills his followers. Geb is healed by a lock of Ra's hair, and he eventually settles down to become a good ruler. When Geb decides to abdicate, he designates Horus as his heir in the north and Set as his heir in the south.

Geb was also sometimes identified as the "Great Cackler," the goose that laid the primordial egg from which the universe emerged. He is therefore sometimes depicted with a goose's head. At other times, he is rendered as a human king, wearing the combined crown of both Upper and Lower Egypt.

Hapy (2; also Hapi)

Associated with the yearly flooding of the Nile, Hapy was one of the most revered gods in the Egyptian pantheon. Hapy was said to live variously in the Underworld or on an island in Elephantine in the First Cataract of the Nile. On the island, Hapy resided in a grotto that was guarded by the god Khnum.

Hapy wears a man's kilt and a headdress of papyrus plants. He is usually represented as an intersex figure, having the beard and hair of a male but the breasts of a female. He also usually has a pot belly. Hapy is portrayed with breasts and a belly because he was considered to be a nurturing, nourishing figure, since life in ancient Egypt was completely dependent on the fecundity brought by the annual floods. Hapy often has blue or green skin, and in the New Kingdom he was sometimes portrayed as a pair of identical gods pulling on the stems of two plants that are entwined together. In this form, Hapy represents the union of Upper and Lower Egypt.

Hapy was intimately linked with Osiris in the Egyptian religious imagination. Just as Osiris returned to life after being dead, Hapy revived Egypt every year with life-giving floodwaters. Osiris was considered to be the god who first taught people how to grow and harvest grain, and since Hapy's floods made agriculture possible, the return of the crops every year was thought to symbolize the resurrection of Osiris. The harvest that followed the floods therefore was both a commemoration and renewal of Osiris's gifts of barley and agriculture.[29]

A surviving hymn to Hapy praises him for his bounty, and it is clear from the text that the time of the Nile floods was an occasion for celebration in ancient Egypt. The hymn also makes clear that inundations that were insufficient or overwhelming might spell disaster, and so Hapy might have a destructive aspect as well as a nurturing one. Below are some excerpts from this hymn, which dates from the Middle Kingdom:[30]

> Hail to you, Hapy,
>
> Sprung from earth,
>
> Come to nourish Egypt!
>
> Of secret ways,
>
> A darkness by day,
>
> To whom his followers sing!
>
> . . . .
>
> When he is sluggish, noses clog,
>
> Everyone is poor;
>
> As the sacred loaves are pared,
>
> A million perish among men.
>
> When he plunders, the whole land rages,
>
> Great and small roar;
>
> People change according to his coming,

---

[29] Pinch, *Handbook*, 137.

[30] Miriam Lichtheim, *Ancient Egyptian Literature: A Book of Readings*, Vol. 1: *The Old and Middle Kingdoms* (Berkeley: University of California Press, 1973), 205–09.

When Khnum has fashioned him.
. . . .
When he rises at the residence,
Men feast on the meadows' gifts,
Decked with lotus for the nose,
And all the things that sprout from the earth.
Children's hands are filled with herbs,
They forget to eat.
Good things are strewn about the houses,
The whole land leaps for joy.
. . . .
Oh joy when you come!
You who feed men and herds
With your meadow gifts!
Oh joy when you come!

Hathor

Hathor is a complex deity who played multiple important roles within Egyptian religion and culture. She was seen as a nurturing cow-goddess, a patron of fertility and motherhood. Hathor also had strong associations with music, dance, drunkenness, and sensuality. As one of the goddesses who represented the Eye of Ra, Hathor had a terrifying, destructive aspect as well. This dual nature as nurturing cow and fierce Eye of Ra is often captured in representations of the goddess, where she is shown as a beautiful woman wearing a headdress of two long, curving cow horns between which is set the sun disk.

Whether Hathor was worshiped in the Predynastic Period is still an open question. Egyptologist Carolyn Graves-Brown notes that "[t]he first clear attestation of Hathor is in the reign of Khafre in the Fourth Dynasty."[31] Once the cult of Hathor became established, however, it became immensely popular. Hathor's primary cult center was at Dendera in central Egypt, but Graves-Brown says that "more temples were built to [Hathor] than to any other Egyptian goddess."[32]

---

[31] Carolyn Graves-Brown, *Dancing for Hathor: Women in Ancient Egypt* (London: Continuum, 2010), 17.

[32] Graves-Brown, *Dancing for Hathor*, xi.

In addition to serving as the Eye of Ra, Hathor was sometimes considered to be Ra's mother and therefore the mother of the pharaoh by extension. This connection was reinforced by images that showed Hathor nursing the pharaoh.[33] The living pharaoh participated in a rite intended to represent him nursing at Hathor's breast. In this rite, the pharaoh would drink from the teats of sacred cows that were kept at the Temple of Hathor. Geraldine Pinch notes that this activity "was part of the coronation ceremony, and seems to have been regularly repeated."[34]

Hathor's motherly role extended beyond the boundaries of life. She was one of the goddesses said to live in the Field of Reeds, which was the Egyptian name for paradise. Just as men were thought to take the name of Osiris upon death, so too did women take the name of Hathor, although the latter was a relatively late development.[35] As a goddess of death, Hathor's duty was to shepherd the soul into the afterlife and see to the soul's comfort. We see this in one prayer found on a cup dating from c. 1550 BCE, where one of the well-wishes for the dead person is "[m]ay Hathor give you beer."[36]

It is Hathor who gives the soul beer because of the goddess's role in the myth of the destruction of humanity. In the myth, Ra is angry because human beings are doing evil things and neglecting the worship of the gods. Ra sends Hathor down to Earth as his Eye to wreak destruction and teach the humans a lesson. Unfortunately, Hathor becomes so wrapped up in this task that she risks destroying all humanity, so the other gods beg Ra to restrain her, otherwise no one will be left to worship them. Ra achieves this by having beer

---

[33] Margaret Bunson, *Encyclopedia of Ancient Egypt*, rev. ed. (New York: Facts on File, Inc., 2002), 160.

[34] Geraldine Pinch, *Magic in Ancient Egypt* (London: British Museum Press, 1994), 83.

[35] Mark Smith, *Following Osiris: Perspectives on the Osirian Afterlife from Four Millennia* (Oxford: Oxford University Press, 2017), 252, 417.

[36] Stephen Quirke, *Exploring Religion in Ancient Egypt* (Chichester: John Wiley

brewed and then colored red. Hathor, who has taken on the guise of the lion-headed goddess Sekhmet, thinks the beer is blood, and she drinks so deeply of it that she passes out drunk. When she wakes up, she is once again restored to her senses.

Beer, drinking, and drunkenness were essential parts of Hathor's feasts. These festivals were also occasions for the expression of joy through music and dance. Hathor was especially associated with the sound of the sistrum, a kind of metallic rattle, and while dance was part of the worship of many Egyptian gods, it was especially connected with Hathor. Graves-Brown notes that dance was sufficiently important to the worship of Hathor that men sometimes danced as well. And not only that, but there were times when the pharaoh himself danced for the goddess.[37]

One aspect of Hathor had particular duties regarding newborn children. This form of Hathor divided her into seven goddesses, and in this form, she visited newborn children and declared what their fates would be. The Seven Hathors could also be called upon in matters of love and were thought to offer protection against demons.[38]

Hathor also participated in the Osiris legend that was central to many Egyptian religious practices. Some scholars think that an older version of the myth cast Hathor in the role of wife to Osiris and mother to Horus, a role that was later taken over by Isis.[39] Hathor plays a different role in a continuation of the Osiris legend known as "The Battle of Horus and Set," wherein the young Horus has to defend his claim to the throne against his evil uncle, the chaos god Set. In this story, Ra and the other gods act as judges who are attempting to figure out whether to grant the crown to Horus or Set. At one point, Ra gets so fed up with the proceedings that he goes into

---

& Sons Ltd., 2010), 69.

[37] Graves-Brown, *Dancing for Hathor*, xi.

[38] Pinch, *Magic in Ancient Egypt*, 37, 81.

[39] See, for example, Hart, *Dictionary*, 62.

his tent by himself to sulk. The other gods discuss what might be done to alleviate Ra's foul mood, and Hathor volunteers to deal with the problem. She goes into Ra's tent, where she takes off her clothes. When Ra sees Hathor's naked body, his good mood is restored, and he returns to his rightful place among the gods.

Hathor's association with Horus continued even after Isis supplanted Hathor as his mother. In some places, Hathor was considered to be the consort of Horus. This was true particularly in Edfu, where a fine temple to Horus was built during the Ptolemaic Period. Egyptologist Rosalie David notes that one annual event at the temple in Edfu involved taking the statue of Hathor from her temple in Dendera and sailing it down the river to Edfu, where ceremonies would be held celebrating the marriage of Hathor and Horus.[40] When the festival was over, the statue would then be sailed back to Dendera and returned to its shrine.

---

[40] A. Rosalie David, *Discovering Ancient Egypt* (New York: Facts on File, 1994), 38.

Horus (Hor, Her, Heru, Har)

Horus is one of the oldest and most complex deities in the Egyptian pantheon and perhaps is one of the most familiar to modern readers. Horus is usually pictured as a falcon, or else as a man with a falcon's head. In either depiction, he is sometimes seen wearing the *pschent* crown of a united Upper and Lower Egypt. At other times, he is shown as a young, winged human boy with his finger raised to his lips; this version of the god was taken up by the Greeks as Harpocrates, the god of the keeping of secrets.

From the beginning of Egyptian history, Horus was a god allied with kingship. The Pre-Dynastic pharaoh Menes, who united Upper and Lower Egypt into a single country, was especially devoted to Horus, which helped to nationalize Horus's cult. However, it was not merely that the king worshiped Horus fervently that united the god with the throne. One primary tenet of Egyptian kingship was that the king himself was a god, and that he specifically was a manifestation or even reincarnation of Horus. This link was cemented when, upon assuming the throne, the king took a new name that was referred to as his "Horus name."

Understanding the nature of Horus is made difficult by the multiplicity of his manifestations. It is unclear whether these were intended to be avatars of the same deity, or whether they were, in fact, separate gods entirely. One version of Horus, often referred to as "Horus the Elder," was said to be the child of the earth god Geb and the sky goddess Nut, making him the brother of Isis, Osiris, Nephthys, and Set. The second version is usually called "Horus the Younger," and in this manifestation, he is the child of Isis and Osiris.

From the earliest times, Horus the Elder was a sky god, whose eyes were the sun and moon. The antiquity of this association with the sky is noted by Egyptologist Geraldine Pinch, who observes that "[o]ne of the earliest divine images known from Egypt is that of a falcon in a barque,"[41] a common ancient Egyptian depiction of the movement of a heavenly body across the sky, which was conceived of as a kind of celestial waterway. In later times, Horus became identified with the sun god Ra, thus assuming a solar aspect himself. Pinch explains that in this manifestation, he was known as "Ra-Horakhty (Ra-Horus of the Double Horizon), who triumphed over his enemies to rise in the east."[42]

Horus the Younger was said to be the child of Isis and Osiris, who was conceived after his father's death through a magical act performed by his mother. In the Osirian myth, Horus is in constant danger from his evil uncle Set, who kills Horus's father not once but twice in an effort to usurp his throne. The manifestation of Horus as the son of Isis and Osiris was commonly co-opted by Egyptian pharaohs at least by the Fifth Dynasty. These pharaohs considered themselves to be both the descendants of Horus and a reincarnation thereof. This association is asserted in the Pyramid Texts, which refer to the pharaoh as Horus when he is a living man and as Osiris once he has died and entered the afterlife.

In addition to the Osirian tale, the other primary myth involving Horus is "The Battle of Horus and Set," a story preserved in a

---

[41] Pinch, *Handbook*, 143.

[42] Pinch, *Handbook*, 144.

papyrus dating from the Twentieth Dynasty. In this tale, Set has usurped the throne of Egypt after the death of Osiris. Horus comes before the supreme god Ra-Horakhty and all the other gods to demand that he be named Osiris's rightful heir. The gods argue back and forth about this. Most of them agree that Horus should be king, but Ra-Horakhty and a few others think that Set should retain the throne because he is older and more experienced. The gods ask for advice from Osiris and from the goddess Neith, both of whom say that Horus should wear the crown.

When the court of the gods fails to reach a consensus, Set suggests a single combat between himself and Horus, with the victor being made king. In the first combat, Set and Horus turn themselves into hippopotamuses to see who can remain under water the longest. Horus's mother Isis tries to rig the contest by harpooning Set, but her first cast goes awry, hitting Horus instead. The second cast hits Set, who rages at his sister for harming him. Isis feels sorry for Set, and so she removes the harpoon, but this angers Horus, who attacks his mother and cuts off her head. Horus then runs off into the mountains with Isis's head, while her body becomes a headless statue. (Later in the story, Isis revives herself.)

Ra-Horakhty demands that Horus pay for his crime, so he sends various gods out to find him. Set comes across Horus while he is sleeping and gouges out his eyes, then denies having seen Horus at all. Horus is later found by Hathor, who heals him and brings him back home. At this point, Ra-Horakhty is so fed up with both Set and Horus that he tells them to go home, eat together, and stop fighting each other.

Set invites Horus home to have a meal with him and to be his guest overnight. Horus agrees, but once he is asleep, Set attempts to rape him. Horus manages to fend Set off, but not before Set has ejaculated into his hands. Later, Set tries to convince the gods that Horus wanted Set to have sex with him and that therefore he is unclean. However, Set is the one who ends up being shamed when his semen calls out to the court of the gods from the river, where Isis had cast Horus's befouled hands (she makes him new ones afterward), and from inside Set's own body, since he had eaten lettuce upon which Isis had secretly poured some of his seed.

Set then proposes another contest. He and Horus are to make boats of stone. Whichever one makes a stone boat that floats on the water gets to be king. Horus cheats by making a boat of plaster and wood that looks like stone, and so wins the contest, upon which Set turns himself into a hippopotamus and rips Horus's boat to shreds.

The suit between Horus and Set is finally decided when Osiris sends one last letter saying that he will harvest the hearts of those who refuse to deal justly with their fellows. This frightens the gods into making a final decision. Set is bound in chains and Horus is made king, at which point Set concedes the throne to him, and the gods rejoice that the issue has finally been decided.

Imhotep (Imouthes)

Deification of rulers, whether during their lifetimes or shortly after their deaths, was a common occurrence in the ancient world. Egyptian kings were thought to be both the offspring and living manifestation of a god, usually Horus or Amen-Ra. It was rather less common for other persons to achieve deified status, although it did happen from time to time. For ancient Egypt, we see this particularly in the person of Imhotep, the vizier of the First Dynasty pharaoh Djoser and probable architect of Djoser's step pyramid in what is now Saqqara. Imhotep eventually was worshiped as a god of wisdom and healing.

Imhotep's glorification and later deification grew out of a tradition of reverence for his wisdom and skill, because the historical Imhotep was a talented, skilled man who was more than worthy of the pharaoh's trust. Over time, Imhotep's legend acquired various accretions. Through these accretions, Imhotep eventually was credited with the authorship of several wisdom texts, was supposed to have been a physician and healer, and was eventually considered to be the son of Ptah, the supreme god of Memphis. Some versions of Imhotep's parentage state that his mother, Khereduankh, was a mortal woman, while others claimed she was the daughter of the god Banebdjedet, which led some people to revere her as a divine being in her own right. A third claim about Imhotep's origins makes him fully divine, stating that he was the son of Ptah and Sekhmet. Alignment of Imhotep with Ptah, rather than with a different deity, stems from Ptah's role as the patron of architects, builders, and craftsmen. In his role as a wise man, Imhotep also became a patron god of scribes.

Accretions to Imhotep's legend and his eventual deification occurred over a very long span of time. References to Imhotep as a glorified or deified figure only appear beginning in the Middle Kingdom, hundreds of years after Imhotep's death. Moreover, legends about Imhotep and various facets of his biography seem to have been created out of whole cloth; there is no evidence that he himself wrote wisdom texts (although one attributed to him does survive) or served as a healer, and his supposed divine or semi-divine status obviously is a work of imagination rather than fact.

One early posthumous reference to Imhotep comes from one of the Harper's Songs. The texts of these songs are sometimes found inscribed in tombs and sometimes on papyrus scrolls. The text of the song in question is preserved in a New Kingdom papyrus, but the language dates it to the Middle Kingdom.[43] In the papyrus, the song is labeled as having been found in the tomb of King Intef, but since several kings used that name, it is impossible to know exactly which one is intended by the label. The song is a meditation on death; below is a brief excerpt:

> Yet those who built tombs,
>
> Their places are gone,
>
> What has become of them?
>
> I have heard the words of Imhotep and Hardedef,
>
> Whose sayings are recited whole.
>
> What of their places?
>
> Their walls have crumbled,

---

[43] Lichtheim, *Literature* 1, 195

> Their places are gone,
>
> As though they had never been!⁴⁴

In this song, we can see that Imhotep is revered but not yet considered a divine being, since the song claims that he is dead.

At least by the reign of Amenhotep III, however, Imhotep was receiving worship in the form of libations. The text of a libation prayer is attested in multiple papyri up through the Late Period.⁴⁵ Further, it is during the Late Period that Imhotep begins to be seen as a divine being, and by the Ptolemaic Period his godhood seems to have been well established.⁴⁶ During the Ptolemaic Period, Imhotep became quite popular among the Greeks, who identified Imhotep with Asclepius, the Greek god of physicians and healing.

Two legends survive that recall Imhotep's deeds. One is a Ptolemaic-era stele that preserves the legend of King Djoser and the famine, which is summarized in the chapter on the god Khnum below. The other tale is much later, having been preserved on a Roman-period papyrus from the Tebtunis Temple Library. Below is a summary of the Tebtunis story by archaeologist Marina Escolano-Poveda:

> This text and other sources describe [Imhotep's] divine father Ptah, his mother Khereduankh, and his sister Renpetneferet, sometimes also referred to as his wife. Imhotep is depicted as a powerful magician in Djoser's royal court. In one episode, he travels to Assyria to recover the 42 limbs of

---

⁴⁴ Lichtheim, *Literature* 1, 196. Hardedef was another wise man from the Old Kingdom who was deified.

⁴⁵ Dietrich Wildung, *Egyptian Saints: Deification in Pharaonic Egypt* (New York: New York University Press, 1977), 34.

⁴⁶ Pinch, *Handbook*, 148

Osiris and fights in a magical contest against an Assyrian sorceress.[47]

In addition to the magical powers attributed to the living Imhotep in the Tebtunis story, other late texts also ascribe to him divine powers after his death and elevation to godhood. A stele carved during the reign of Cleopatra VII was made in memory of Taimhotep, wife of the high priest of Ptah at Memphis. Part of the stele is devoted to the story of how Taimhotep was finally able to give her husband a male heir, which she achieved after she and her husband prayed together to Imhotep, "the god great in wonders, effective in deeds, who gives a son to him who has none."[48] That the cult of Imhotep was both popular and important is also shown by the preservation of a hymn addressed to him in the Temple of Ptah at Karnak, which was located next to the great temple to Amen-Ra, one of the most important religious centers in all of ancient Egypt.

---

[47] Marina Escolano-Poveda, "Imhotep: A Sage Between Fiction and Reality," American Research Center in Egypt website, accessed 23 June 2020, https://www.arce.org/resource/imhotep-sage-between-fiction-and-reality.

[48] Miriam Lichtheim, *Ancient Egyptian Literature: A Book of Readings*, Vol. 3: *The Late Period* (Berkeley: University of California Press, 1980), 62.

Isis

The goddess Isis is one of the Egyptian deities most familiar to people today. Originally a goddess of fertility, motherhood, and childbirth, Isis was also considered to be an ancestor of the pharaohs of Egypt, who were thought to be both the direct descendants of Isis's son, Horus, and manifestations of Horus himself. Isis was associated with magic and with healing, and many surviving prayers and magic spells call upon her for aid. Isis appears to have been a relatively obscure goddess in the Early Dynastic Period (also known as the Archaic Period), which began c. 3100 BCE, but she became one of the most important and enduring figures of the Egyptian pantheon. After the conquest of Egypt by Alexander the Great, the Greeks and Romans also began to worship Isis, constructing their own rites and mysteries around her cult. Even today, some modern pagans worship Isis and create rituals around her myth.

The earliest apparent reference to Isis may be on a tablet made by Hor-Aha, an early First Dynasty pharaoh of the Archaic Period. This tablet refers to "Sothis, Opener of the Year, Inundation 1," which might be a reference to Isis because she was often linked with Sothis, the star that we know today as Sirius, whose rising always signaled the flooding of the Nile, an event that was vital to ancient Egyptian agriculture.[49]

Otherwise, the first written references to Isis date from the next major period in ancient Egyptian history, the Old Kingdom, and more specifically from the Fifth Dynasty. These references appear in writings known collectively as the Pyramid Texts, which are inscriptions on the walls of the tombs of some of the pharaohs of Egypt and their queens in what is now Saqqara, Egypt, which originally had been the Egyptian capital of Memphis. The earliest Pyramid Texts are in the tomb of Unas, who ruled Egypt between c. 2375 and c. 2345 BCE. However, Egyptologist James P. Allen states that the somewhat archaic form of the language used for the texts in Unas's tomb suggests that they may in fact be much older.[50]

In all of the Pyramid Texts, Isis functions as one of the deities who cares for the soul of the pharaoh as it makes its transition into the afterlife. For example, texts in the pyramid of Unas depict Isis offering her breast for the soul of Unas to suckle and asking her to bring him back to life, just as she did for her husband/brother, Osiris.[51] Isis also performs similar services for the other kings and queens whose tombs preserve these texts, most of which date from the Sixth Dynasty, although one dates from the Eighth.

Egyptologist Susan Tower Hollis observes parallels between Isis's role as a guide into the afterlife with the role of human women who prepared the bodies for burial. Like human women, Isis is not alone in her task; in the Pyramid Texts she is consistently paired with her sister, Nephthys.[52] Hollis notes further that the familiar story of

---

[49] Normandi Ellis, *Feasts of Light: Celebrations for the Seasons of Life Based on the Egyptian Goddess Mysteries* (Wheaton: The Theosophical Publishing House, 1999), 3.

[50] Allen, *Pyramid Texts*, 4.

[51] Allen, *Pyramid Texts*, 20, 35.

[52] Susan Tower Hollis, *Five Egyptian Goddesses: Their Possible Beginnings, Actions, and Relationships in the Third Millennium BCE* (n.c.: Bloomsbury

Osiris's death and Isis's subsequent search for and resurrection of his body is primarily retained not in ancient Egyptian sources but in the works of the Roman historian and scholar Plutarch, whose *De Iside et Osiride* ("Concerning Isis and Osiris") was written in the second century CE.[53]

Isis's connection to Egyptian royal authority is attested in part by the use of a throne as a sort of headdress in many ancient Egyptian visual representations of the goddess. Indeed, her name in Egyptian is *Eset*, which literally means "seat" or "throne." However, this is not the only way in which Isis is depicted. During the New Kingdom, Isis begins to be shown wearing a crown of cow's horns that hold up a sun disk, attesting to the conflation of Isis with the cow-goddess Hathor, an earlier Egyptian goddess whose popularity waned as that of Isis grew.

Although Isis was hailed as a goddess of fertility, especially with reference to the annual flooding of the Nile that brought in the rich silt that made farming possible in Egypt's arid desert climate, she was not herself a creator goddess but rather the great-great-granddaughter of the original creator god, Atum.

According to the myth of Isis and Osiris, Osiris becomes the ruler of Egypt, teaching people agriculture and law. When Seth becomes jealous of Osiris's power, he creates a chest made precisely to Osiris's measurements. Seth tricks Osiris into getting into the chest and then dumps it into the Nile, where it floats all the way to the Delta. When the chest washes up on the shore, a tamarisk tree grows around it. The tree is later felled by the king of Byblos, who uses it in the construction of his house.

Distraught at Osiris's disappearance, Isis goes searching for him. She eventually locates the tree—now being used as a pillar—and manages to free Osiris from it. By this time, Osiris is dead, so Isis

---

Publishing, 2019), n.p. Accessed on Google Books, http://www.google.com/books.
[53] Hollis, *Five Egyptian Goddesses*, n.p.

carries his body to a swamp, where she hides from the vengeful Seth. Seth eventually finds the hiding place while Isis is away and dismembers Osiris's body, scattering the pieces throughout the land.

Once again, Isis goes looking for her husband, this time with the help of her sister, Nephthys. The sisters manage to find and reconnect all the parts of Osiris's body except his penis, which has landed in the Nile and has been eaten by a fish. Osiris comes back to life through the force of Isis's magic, but because his body is incomplete, he can no longer stay among the living; he has become a mummy, and thus he passes into the Underworld to become the lord of the dead. Isis then gives birth to Horus, the son Osiris gives her when she magically removes his seed from him while she is in the form of a kite, a small bird of prey.

In this myth, we can see many connections between Isis and various aspects of Egyptian life and religion. The myth designates her as the originator of mummification and a participant in funerary rites along with her sister, Nephthys; her magic allows the dead to return to life and to move into the Underworld, a role that she is repeatedly called upon to play in funerary writings such as the Pyramid Texts; and she becomes the mother of the royal houses of Egypt through her son, Horus.

For all her importance to Egyptian religion and funerary practices, Isis did not have a temple of her own until fairly late, and even then, most of those temples were built by rulers who were not themselves Egyptians. The earliest temple to Isis was erected c. 690 BCE by the Cushite pharaoh Taharqa in Philae, an important sacred center near the First Cataract of the Nile. The temple at Philae was enlarged by Nectanebo II, the last Egyptian pharaoh, in the mid-fourth century BCE, but otherwise the rest of the construction was overseen by non-Egyptians, including some of the Hellenistic rulers during the Ptolemaic Period and then later by the Roman emperors Augustus, Tiberius, and Hadrian.

The temple complex at Philae remained in use for the worship of Isis until the middle of the sixth century CE, when it was converted into a Christian church by Byzantine Emperor Justinian I (527-565 CE). In modern times, the temple complex was removed to an island in the middle of Lake Nasser because of damage from the flooding caused by the Aswan Dam. The temple underwent heavy restoration work as part of the moving process, and was reopened to the public in 1980.

The end of nearly three thousand years of Egyptian dynastic rule, beginning with the Persian conquest in 343 BCE, had important effects on Egyptian religious practices. A succession of Persian kings held sway over Egypt until 332 BCE, when the Macedonian military leader Alexander the Great swooped in and took over the country. Alexander's conquest set in motion the Hellenization of Egypt, a process that gained steam after 309 BCE, when the Macedonian Argead succession came to an abrupt end with the assassination of Alexander's son. After a brief interregnum, a Greek companion of Alexander's took the throne of Egypt as Ptolemy I Soter ("Ptolemy the Savior") in 305 BCE.

Ptolemy's accession ushered in a period of alteration of Egyptian culture through the importation of Greek rulers and Greek immigrants. This influx of Greek culture influenced certain aspects of Egyptian culture and religious practices, despite the support of the Ptolemaic rulers for native Egyptian religious expression, and despite Egyptian resentment toward their Greek overlords. The Roman conquest of Egypt in 30 BCE created additional ties between Egypt and the Roman Empire, ensuring interplay between Roman and Egyptian culture as well.

One outcome of this exchange among Egyptian, Greek, and Roman cultures was the growth of the Isis cult, which found sturdy footholds in both Greece and Rome, although acceptance of the worship of Egyptian deities in Rome initially met with some official governmental resistance.[54] Alexander's capital city of Alexandria, situated on Egypt's Mediterranean coast along the northwestern edge of the Nile Delta, was a prominent locus for the growth of this cult. Alexandria's strategic location, economic power, and reputation as a seat of learning made it an ideal place for people from Greece and other parts of the ancient world to do business and to start new lives, and part of that process was the adoption and transformation of local religious ideas and practices.

However, the Hellenic expansion of the Isis cult was not entirely organic. Ptolemy I recognized the need to integrate Greek and Egyptian religious practices, and so he commanded two priests, Manetho, a native Egyptian, and Timotheus, the son of Greek immigrants, to help align the two religions and smooth over the places where important conceptions about the various deities were in conflict.[55] Historian R. E. Witt reports that the result of Manetho and Timotheus's collaboration was the elevation of Isis and her son Horus to the status of Alexandria's primary deities, with Anubis following close behind. But a mother goddess is nothing without a consort, so a new deity named Serapis (or Sarapis) was created, both as an outgrowth of the cult of the Apis bull at Memphis and as a syncretization of aspects of Greek deities, such as Zeus and Hades, with aspects of Egyptian deities, such as Osiris and Amen.[56]

Isis herself underwent a process of syncretization. Ancient Greek writers such as Diodorus Siculus and Herodotus identified her with Demeter, while Plutarch aligned her with Demeter's daughter, Persephone.[57] Historian Vincent Arieh Tobin states that the

---

[54] Herwig Maehler, "Roman Poets on Egypt," in *Ancient Perspectives on Egypt*, ed. by Roger Matthews and Cornelia Roemer (London: UCL Press, 2003), 205.

[55] R. E. Witt, *Isis in the Ancient World* (Baltimore: Johns Hopkins University Press, 1971), 52.

[56] Witt, *Isis in the Ancient World*, 52–53.

[57] Vincent Arieh Tobin, "Isis and Demeter: Symbols of Divine Motherhood," *Journal of the American Research Center in Egypt* 28 (1991): 187–8.

identification of Isis with Demeter has to do in part with the roles of both Demeter and Isis as goddesses of fertility and, in particular, with their association with grain crops, while author Joshua J. Mark suggests that it is the journey of each goddess to find a deceased loved one that linked the two in the minds of ancient Greeks.[58]

However the goddess Isis was perceived by worshipers or her identity shaped for public perception by rulers, it is undeniable that her cult became one of the most important in many locations throughout the Mediterranean Basin during the Ptolemaic Period. We can see her importance in the Isis aretalogy, or list of deeds, from Cyme in Asia Minor, which was probably written sometime in the second century CE by a Greek named Demetrius, who claimed to have copied it from a stele at the temple of Hephaestus in Memphis. In the excerpt from the aretalogy given below, Isis claims to be the daughter of the Greek god Kronos and is elevated to the status of a creator goddess as well as an establisher of order and ruler over various aspects of nature:

> I gave and ordained laws for men, which no one is able to change.
>
> I am eldest daughter of Kronos.
>
> I am wife and sister of King Osiris.
>
> I am she who findeth fruit for men.
>
> I am mother of King Horus.
>
> I am she that riseth in the Dog Star
>
> For me was the city of Bubastis built.
>
> I divided the earth from the heaven.
>
> I showed the paths of the stars.
>
> I ordered the course of the sun and the moon.

---

[58] Tobin, "Isis and Demeter," 188; Joshua J. Mark, "Isis," *Ancient History Encyclopedia*, 19 February 2016, https://www.ancient.eu/isis/.

I devised business in the sea.[59]

In addition to syncretizing Egyptian and Greek deities, Hellenized worship of Isis, along with its eventual Roman expression, took the form of a mystery cult similar to the Eleusinian Mysteries, which were celebrated in honor of the Greek goddess Demeter. Mystery cults had extensive rules for how one might become an initiate and complex rituals that guided the practice of initiation and worship. Information about the shape of the mysteries of Isis survives in the *Metamorphoses* by Apuleius, a Numidian writing in Latin in the second century CE. Apuleius's *Metamorphoses* is also known as *The Golden Ass*, after the central misfortune of the protagonist, Lucius, who is turned into a donkey. Lucius is later restored to his human form by the goddess Isis, whereupon he becomes an initiate in the mysteries of that goddess. Historian Antonía Tripolitis provides this summary of the mysteries according to Apuleius:

> [I]nitiation into the Isaic cult was limited to individuals who were selected by Isis herself and who were able to afford the high expenses involved in the initiation. These individuals were notified of the honor by Isis in a dream. Prior to the initiation, the individual underwent a bath of purification and 10 days of strict fasting. The initiate was then dressed in a linen robe and permitted to enter the sanctuary where he/she wandered in the dark places of the underworld and underwent certain trials. The morning after the initiation, the initiate, standing on a wooden podium before the statue of Isis, was

---

[59] Reprinted in Marvin W. Meyer, ed., *The Ancient Mysteries: A Sourcebook* (San Francisco: Harper & Row, 1987), 173.

presented to the crowd. This day was considered a new birthday for the initiate. It signified that he/she had died to the old life and was reborn to a new course of life and salvation under the protection of Isis.[60]

Worship of Isis was not completely relegated to mystery cults in the Greco-Roman world, however. Every year in March, beginning in the first century CE, the Romans celebrated a public festival called *Navigium Isidis* ("the Ship of Isis").[61] During this festival, which marked the official start to the sailing season, a special boat consecrated to Isis would be launched into the sea in a petition for the goddess's protection of sailors, fishermen, and all those who traveled the waves.[62]

Although the cult of Isis waned as time progressed, it did not disappear entirely. In the eighteenth century, Wolfgang Amadeus Mozart referred to aspects of the Isis mystery cult in his opera *The Magic Flute*, in which the lead character, Tamino, must undergo a series of trials in order to win entry into the Temple of Light, and in which a hymn to Isis and Osiris is sung. More recently, modern pagans have adopted Isis as a deity worthy of reverence. Authors such as Normandi Ellis and de Traci Regula have written books explaining the history of the Isis cult and demonstrating how modern devotees might adapt the worship of Isis to their own spiritual needs.[63]

From her humble beginnings as a native Egyptian funerary goddess and patron of fertility and motherhood, Isis rose to significantly

---

[60] Antonía Tripolitis, *Religions of the Hellenistic-Roman Age* (Grand Rapids: William B. Eerdmans Publishing Company, 2002), 29.

[61] Laurent Bricault, *Isis Pelagia: Images, Names and Cults of a Goddess of the Seas,* trans. Gil H. Renberg (Leiden: Brill, 2020), 222.

[62] Bricault, *Isis Pelagia,* 228.

[63] de Traci Regula, *The Mysteries of Isis: Her Worship and Magick* (St. Paul: Llewellyn Publications, 2001); Ellis, *Feasts of Light*.

greater stature in the Greco-Roman world than she had held in her own native Egypt. This may be so because it is easy to identify with the goddess's struggles in her myth: her sorrow at the death of her spouse and desire to raise him from the dead, her attempts to protect her young son, and her connection with human aspects of life and death through the agricultural cycle and funerary rites. It is no surprise, therefore, that unlike many other ancient deities, Isis has remained a vivid character in the human imagination even five centuries after she first began to be worshiped along the banks of the Nile.

Khnum (Chnum)

Khnum was the god of the source of the Nile, and in some myths was considered to be a creator god. Khnum is usually pictured as a man with the head of a ram. The horns of this ram do not curl in a spiral but rather are wavy and extend out horizontally to the left and right over the ram's head. The primary cult centers for Khnum were at Elephantine, an island in the Nile River just downstream from the First Cataract, and Esna, which is on the west bank of the Nile, south of Luxor.

The identity of Khnum's consort varied depending on location. At Elephantine, Khnum was said to be the husband of Satis, the goddess of war, hunting, and fertility, and the father of Anuket, the goddess of the cataracts of the Nile. At Esna, Khnum's consort was variously Neith or Menhit, who were both war goddesses (although Neith was considerably more popular and powerful), and Khnum's son was Heka, the god of medicine and magic. Khnum was also associated with Hapy, the god of the Nile floods, and was said to be a manifestation of the soul of the sun god, Ra. When Khnum was acting in that capacity, he carried the name Khnum-Ra.

In addition to ensuring the annual flooding of the Nile, Khnum also created the world out of nothing and formed the first human beings on his potter's wheel. He made men and women out of clay and breathed life into them, giving each person a *ba*, or soul. A surviving hymn to Khnum from the temple at Esna details his act of creation, listing various body parts along with their functions, and also stating that Khnum made the plants and the animals.[64]

Although Khnum was worshiped primarily at Elephantine and Esna, he was known and revered throughout Egypt. He is mentioned in the Pyramid Texts, which date from the Fifth Dynasty and which are written on tombs near Saqqara, at the base of the Nile Delta at the opposite end of the river from Khnum's main cult centers. For example, Khnum is said to have built a ferryboat for the pharaoh Unas, and he is credited with having created the pharaoh Teti.[65]

Khnum's importance as a creator and controller of the Nile floods was occasionally harnessed for political purposes. When Queen Hatshepsut assumed the throne following the death of her husband, Pharaoh Thutmose II, she promulgated the myth that Amen was her father and that her body and soul were made by Khnum himself, as part of an effort to legitimize her rule.

Another myth states that when a famine descended upon the land, Pharaoh Djoser had a dream wherein Khnum appeared to him and promised to make the Nile flood so that the famine would stop. In thanks for the god's help, Djoser gave a grant of land and yearly tithes to be paid to Khnum's temple. It is unclear whether the story about Djoser actually dates from the Third Dynasty, since it is preserved on a stele that dates from Ptolemaic times. It is possible that the story is actually from Ptolemaic Egypt but was forged to make it seem older, in order to give it more weight and importance.

---

[64] Lichtheim, *Literature* 3, 112–13.
[65] Allen, *Pyramid Texts*, pp. 55, 68.

Khonsu (Khons, Chons)

Khonsu, whose name means "traveler," was the Egyptian god of the moon. He is usually depicted as a mummy with a child's shaved head and braided sidelock, although sometimes he is shown as a man with a falcon's head wearing a headdress in which the moon disk is set. One of Khonsu's main cult centers was the city of Thebes. In Thebes, as well as in the rest of southern Egypt, Khonsu was part of the Theban Triad, in which the god Amen was Khonsu's father and the goddess Mut was his mother. Within the great temple of Amen in Karnak, Khonsu has his own precinct. In the northern part of Egypt, however, Khonsu was in a triad with his parents Ptah and Sekhmet, while in the Fayum, his parents were said to be Hathor and Sobek.

As a moon good, Khonsu was sometimes associated with Thoth, and therefore was seen as a god of calendars and timekeeping. In the myth of the birth of the children of Nut, Khonsu loses at dice to Thoth, and as a result, he has to forfeit a fifth of his light. Thoth uses that light to make the five intercalary days that were added to the 360-day lunar calendar in order to keep it aligned with the seasons.

Egyptologist Geraldine Price notes that the earliest mentions of Khonsu paint him as a god to be feared, because he "strangled lesser deities and ate the hearts of the dead."[66] He was also feared because of his role as Keeper of the Books of the End of the Year, a list of all the people who were destined to die during that year.[67] When Khonsu played that role, he was thought to take on the shape of a baboon, another aspect that he shares with Thoth.

Sometimes Khonsu's ferocity was called upon to cast out demons and heal the sick. We see this in one of the primary myths about Khonsu, which is preserved in a fourth-century BCE inscription that details how he healed a princess from demonic possession. In the story, a princess from a country called Bekhten becomes very ill because a demon has taken hold of her. Pharaoh Rameses II, who is married to the princess's sister, is asked for help, so he sends his learned men to Bekhten to see what might be done. The most learned and skilled of all these wise men tries his best to cure the young woman, but soon discovers that he has no power over the demon. The learned men return home, sorrowful that they could not help.

When Rameses hears what happened, he goes to the Temple of Khonsu to ask for aid. The priests of the temple suggest taking a statue of the god to Bekhten so that the god can fight the demon. Khonsu agrees to go, so Rameses sends him to Bekhten with a great retinue, and the god is immediately brought before the afflicted princess. Khonsu has a conversation with the demon, who demands that the people of Bekhten hold a festival in his honor if they want him to leave. Khonsu decides that this is a reasonable request and agrees to the demon's terms. The king of Bekhten also agrees, and so the demon leaves, after which the king holds the feast as he promised. Once the festival is completed, the princess is well again, upon which the king orders another festival, this time to celebrate the princess's return to health and to give thanks to Khonsu for his help.

---

[66] Pinch, *Handbook*, 155.

[67] Pinch, *Handbook*, 155.

After the festival of thanksgiving, the Egyptian priests ask leave to depart, but the king doesn't want them to go because he's afraid the demon might come back once Khonsu leaves. The priests then make a shrine for Khonsu in Bekhten, where he is greatly honored. The priests and Khonsu spend three years in Bekhten, at the end of which the god appears to the king in a dream and tells him that he wants to go home. The king is saddened by this, but he understands what he must do. He gives the priests many gifts for themselves and other treasures besides for them to put in Khonsu's temple in Egypt. The priests take the god home, and everyone lives in peace thereafter.

Maat (Ma'at, Ma'et, Mayet)

The goddess Maat was the personification of justice, law, cosmic order, and right living, and as such was one of the most important deities in the Egyptian pantheon. She is often portrayed as a beautiful woman wearing a dress and a headband in which an ostrich feather has been placed. Maat was not only a goddess, however; as a moral, religious, and legal concept, *maat* played a vital role in Egyptian kingship and in the daily life of all Egyptians. Egyptologist Geraldine Pinch notes that "[t]he primary duty of an Egyptian king was to be the champion of *maat*. In the afterlife, the dead were judged on whether they had done and spoken *maat*."[68] This judgment was accomplished by weighing the heart of the deceased person against the goddess Maat's ostrich feather. A just heart would be equal in weight to the feather, or even lighter, while an evil heart would be heavier. The person with a just heart would be allowed to go on to paradise, while those who had evil hearts were consumed by Ammit.

Maat was usually seen as the wife of Thoth and the daughter of Ra, and was said to travel with Ra in his solar barge. Author Veronica Ions notes that Maat, when part of the crew of Ra's barque, represented

---

[68] Pinch, *Handbook*, 159.

"[t]he light which Ra brought into the world ... he created the world by putting her in the place of chaos."[69]

But Maat was more than Ra's creature: she was also the basis for Ra's own power. Visual representations of this sometimes show Ra sitting on a small plinth, which represents Maat. Maat is the foundation upon which Ra sits, and therefore, she represents the foundation of cosmic order. The depiction of Maat as a plinth that supports a god is not limited to Ra. Osiris and Ptah are also frequently shown standing on this platform, which visually reinforced their own authority and dedication to justice and order.

---

[69] Veronica Ions, *Egyptian Mythology* (New York: Peter Bedrick Books, 1990), 113.

Nefertem (Nefertum)

The word "nefer" means "beautiful" in ancient Egyptian, and the god Nefertem was associated particularly with the beauty of the lotus flower. Because of the lotus's sweet scent, Nefertem was also the god of perfumes. In the Memphite Triad, Nefertem was the son of Ptah and Sekhmet. Nefertem is often depicted as a beautiful young man, sometimes with the head of a lion, with a lotus flower headdress. Because of this association with the lotus, Nefertem was also connected in the Egyptian religious imagination to aspects of the creation of the universe and to the creator god Ra.

One ancient Egyptian creation story says that, in the beginning, there was only a lotus floating on the waters of Nun. When the lotus opened, the sun god Ra was born from inside it. Egyptologist Geraldine Pinch states that the connection between the sun and the lotus flower in this creation myth likely comes from observations of the lotus's behavior. It only opens during the day, and it is pollinated by beetles, an insect that was considered to be a form of Khepera, the god of the rising sun.[70]

---

[70] Pinch, *Handbook*, 158.

Neith (Neit)

The goddess Neith had her primary cult center in the city of Sais in the Nile Delta. Her name seems to mean "the terrifying one," and her primary symbol appears to represent two arrows crossed over a shield. These attributes suggest that she originally was a warlike deity. Neith is sometimes depicted as a woman wearing a dress, with the cartouche-shaped symbol just mentioned on her head, while at other times she is shown wearing the red crown of Lower Egypt. She was a goddess of weaving, mothers, and wisdom, and she was also considered to be a creator deity.

In her role as a creator, Neith had nonbinary gender. Geraldine Pinch states that Neith was referred to as "Mother and Father of All Things," a deity who "created the world by speaking seven magical words."[71] This version of the creation myth is preserved at the Temple of Khnum at Esna. In this myth, Neith emerges from the primeval waters, creates the primeval mound, and then speaks creation into being.[72]

---

[71] Pinch, *Handbook*, 170.

[72] Barbara Watterson, *The Gods of Ancient Egypt* (New York: Facts on File, Inc., 1984), 176.

Neith was the mother of the crocodile god Sobek and was considered to be one of the great mother goddesses of Egypt. She was respected for her wisdom, and in the myth "The Battle of Horus and Set," the gods appeal to her to settle the dispute over who should be the king of Egypt. Her reply in support of Horus is curt and no-nonsense, as is the wont of older women who are fed up with the squabbling of children.

Nephthys (Nebt-het)

Nephthys was the daughter of the earth god Geb and the sky goddess Nut. Even though she was the sister to Isis, Osiris, and Set, Nephthys often takes on a secondary role in most myths. However, her role is still very important; it is with Nephthys's help that Isis is able to reassemble the pieces of her dismembered husband and bring him back to life. For this reason, Nephthys was associated with death and funerals, and she is often depicted standing alongside the bier with Isis. Further, as a goddess of weaving, Nephthys was specifically associated with the weaving of linen wrappings for mummies.

Nephthys was nominally married to her brother Set, just as Isis was paired off with Osiris. Nephthys's marriage does not seem to have been a happy one; at one point she seduces Osiris, and Anubis is born from that union. Nephthys is more commonly depicted as spending time with Isis rather than Set in both myths and various ancient illustrations of mythical scenes.

Together with Isis, Nephthys had the function of a mourner at a funeral. This is shown in the funerary texts mentioned above, but especially in a surviving text known as "The Lamentations of Isis and Nephthys," in which the two goddesses mourn for the slain Osiris. This text came to be performed during rites commemorating the death of Osiris, and it eventually came to be included as part of the *Book of the Dead.*

Nun (Noun, Nu)

To the ancient Egyptians, Nun was simultaneously a place, a substance, a concept, and a deity. Nun was the primordial waters from which all creation arose, both as the substance of the waters themselves and as the place where those waters resided. Nun was the place in which the universe began and a place that continued to exist even after the world was made. The creator god Atum came into being in the middle of Nun, and it is in Nun that he gave birth to his children Shu and Tefnut, the air and the light of the world. As a concept, Nun represented insubstantiality and formlessness, while as a deity, Nun was the frog-headed personification of both the primordial waters and of formlessness, existing alongside his snake-headed consort Naunet as part of the Hermopolitan Ogdoad, the collection of eight deities who arose from nothingness to undertake the first acts of creation.

Nun was not just a god of the past, nor did Nun cease to be of cosmological importance once the world was created. Even after the universe had been brought fully to life, Nun played important roles in the Egyptian understanding of how the world worked. Nun flowed through the Underworld, and Nun was the origin of the waters of the Nile. Various deities and demons dwelt in Nun, from where they could arise to help or hinder humans. For example, the great serpent

Apep (Apophis) dwelt in Nun and had to be vanquished every night lest he devour the sun as it made its transit from west to east on the waters of the Underworld, and when the boat of Ra made that transit safely, some myths claimed that it was the waters of Nun that raised up the sun in the morning.

In addition to the omnipresent Nile, other waters were used as physical representations of Nun in ancient Egyptian religious architecture and practice. For example, because the vulture goddess Nekhebet also inhabited Nun, her temple at Elkab had a sacred lake representing the primordial waters.

Waters representing Nun were an important part of the pharaoh's daily routine. Every morning when the pharaoh arose, a ceremony called the "Rite of the House of Morning" was performed, in which the pharaoh was bathed and dressed for the day. The water used for the bathing was taken from a sacred source and represented Nun. Being bathed in the waters of Nun was thought to represent the rebirth of the pharaoh, an echo of Ra's journey across Nun in the Underworld to be reborn every morning as the rising sun. In this way, the pharaoh's body was aligned with that of Ra and made to participate in the god's own activities.

The Ogdoad of Hermopolis

The Ogdoad was a set of eight primeval gods worshiped at Khemenu in central Egypt. Khemenu literally means "Eight Town," a reference to the Ogdoad, but today we are more familiar with its Greek name: Hermopolis ("City of Hermes"). The Ogdoad was made up of four pairs of deities, with each pair consisting of a god and his consort. The gods were usually depicted as men with frogs' heads, while the goddesses were shown as women with serpents' heads. Each divine pair represented a different cosmic concept, as described in the table below:

Deities	Concept
Amen and Amaunet	Hiddenness
Heh and Hauhet	Eternity
Kek and Kekhet	Darkness
Nun and Naunet	Primeval waters

According to the Hermopolitan creation story, these eight deities created the world out of a primeval mound that stood in the waters of Nun. These primordial waters were represented by a sacred lake at the main temple in Hermopolis, and a small island in the middle of the lake was said to be the primeval mound itself. The myth goes on to state that once the Ogdoad had created the world, they ruled over it for a time, then died and went into the Underworld, where they continued to cause the Nile to flow and the sun to rise.

Although the Ogdoad were important creator deities in Hermopolis, the Hermopolitan creation myth in fact had four other variants:

> A celestial goose called the "Great Cackler" lays an egg on the primeval mound; the egg contains the god Ra, who then goes on to create the world.
>
> Similar to the first version, but the bird laying the cosmic egg is an ibis, representing the god Thoth (identified with Hermes by the Greeks, which is the origin of the name "Hermopolis").
>
> A lotus flower rises out of the primeval waters, and when it opens, Ra is born from inside it.
>
> Similar to the third version, but it is a scarab beetle inside the lotus, and when the beetle weeps, humans are created.

Of the deities in the Ogdoad, Amen and Nun both went on to have important places in the mythology and religion of Egypt as a whole, while the others were worshiped primarily at Hermopolis.

Osiris

Osiris, the dying and rising god, was one of the most important deities in the Egyptian pantheon. The eldest child of the sky goddess Nut and the earth god Geb, Osiris was credited with bringing civilization to human beings, teaching them agriculture and law, and giving them grain to grow and eat. Osiris was both the brother and the husband of the goddess Isis, who assisted him in his work during his life. Following his dismemberment by his jealous brother Set and his later resurrection by Isis, Osiris descended into the Tuat, or Underworld, where he became the god of the dead and the judge of souls.

Osiris's name in Egyptian is *Usir*, which means "powerful." ("Osiris" is a Latin version of the name.) Osiris was closely associated with the agricultural cycle, and especially with the risings and fallings of the Nile, upon which all Egyptian agriculture depended. In his guise as the god of the dead, Osiris is often depicted as having green skin and swathed in a mummy's bands, wearing the white, feathered *atef* crown and holding the scepter and flail that were the symbols of Egyptian kingship. The greenness of his skin is not connected to death, but rather is a reference to his lifegiving power through his control of the inundations of the Nile. Other representations of Osiris show him as a normal human being, dressed as an Egyptian pharaoh.

The primary Osiris myth states that when Osiris ruled over Egypt long, long ago, his brother Seth became jealous of his power and arranged to kill him by sealing him inside a specially made coffin and tossing it into the Nile. The coffin washes up on the shores of the city of Byblos, where it becomes lodged in the roots of a growing tamarisk tree. When the tamarisk is fully grown, the king of Byblos cuts it down to use as a pillar in his palace, completely unaware of the god concealed inside. Osiris's sister-wife, Isis, goes on a journey looking for her husband. She manages to locate the tamarisk tree and free Osiris's body from it. With the help of other gods, she resurrects Osiris, but this second life doesn't last long. Seth finds Osiris and kills him again, this time chopping his body up into fourteen pieces that he scatters throughout the land. Isis goes looking for the pieces of her husband's body, and she finds all but the penis, which had been thrown into the Nile and devoured by a fish. Isis puts Osiris back together by mummifying his body, but this time he cannot stay in the land of the living; he instead goes down into the Tuat, where he reigns as king.

The origins of the Osiris cult are both ancient and complex. It is often assumed that he has his origins in the ancient city of Djedu in the Nile Delta, where he may have been conflated with a local fertility god named Andjeti.[73] Originally, Osiris was a relatively minor god, considered secondary to the sun god, Ra, but as time wore on, Osiris gradually eclipsed Ra in some respects and became one of the primary deities of the Egyptian pantheon. This change did not take place overnight; although it is possible Osiris was worshiped in the earlier dynasties of the Old Kingdom, it is not until the Fifth Dynasty Pyramid Texts that we see him being treated as the lord of the dead and facilitator of the resurrection of the king. It is also during the Fifth Dynasty that we see Osiris's new importance within Egyptian religion.

---

[73] Ions, *Egyptian Mythology*, 126.

Egyptologist Rosalie David notes that as the Osiris cult grew in popularity, there was a shift in the Egyptian understanding of the afterlife. According to David, paradise was initially accessible only by the pharaohs, but during the Middle Kingdom, this exclusive club was opened to other Egyptian nobles.[74] The democratization of the afterlife continued until eventually people from all walks of life were thought to be able to enter into paradise if they had lived good lives.

The Osiris cult, once established, was centered primarily in the southern city of Abydos, near the modern-day town of El Bayana, with a less important shrine in the city of Busiris (now Abu Sir Bana) in the central Nile Delta. Abydos was traditionally thought to be the place where Osiris's head landed after his dismemberment by Set, and Busiris the place to which Set flung Osiris's spine. Located along the Nile in Upper Egypt, Abydos had a number of temple complexes and also a royal necropolis, which was used for the burials of early pharaohs. Burial in a place sacred to Osiris likely reflected the wish that the person being buried would be resurrected just as the god had been.

According to Egyptologist E. A. Wallace Budge, the temple at Abydos was constructed during the Twelfth Dynasty at the command of Pharaoh Senusret III.[75] Budge notes that a description of this temple survives in the text of a stele made by Ikhernefert, the official commissioned with its construction. In addition to the temple building, which the stele reports was made "from sweet-smelling woods, and inlaid with gold, silver, and lapis-lazuli," Ikhernefert caused a new statue of the god and a new neshmet boat to be made. The neshmet boat was both the sacred boat in which Osiris sailed in his journey through the Underworld, as described in the *Book of the*

---

[74] A. Rosalie David, *The Ancient Egyptians: Religious Beliefs and Practices* (London: Routledge & Kegan Paul, 1982), 73.

[75] E. A. Wallace Budge, *Osiris and the Egyptian Resurrection*, vol. 2 (London: P. L. Warner, [1911]), 4.

Dead, and also a physical object in the world of the living, which was a part of sacred processions in honor of the god.[76]

A basic outline of some of the rites of Osiris also survives on the stele of Ikhernefert. Ikhernefert says that the statue of the god was richly dressed and placed inside its neshmet boat, which then was taken on a long procession that involved several stages that occurred as follows:[77]

1. A procession involving the jackal-headed funerary god Wepwawet (not to be confused with Anubis), who functioned during this festival as a stand-in for or avatar of Osiris's son, Horus
2. A mock attack on Osiris's neshmet boat as it leaves its sanctuary in Abydos, in which the attackers are repelled
3. The procession of the neshmet boat moves eastward from Abydos to Peqer (now Umm Al Qa'ab), the location of the royal necropolis, representing Osiris's death
4. Another mock battle on the riverbank, in which Osiris's followers are victorious (although the ancient historian Herodotus claims that sometimes these mock battles descended into actual violence) 78
5. A procession to return the neshmet boat to Abydos

---

[76] Budge, *Egyptian Resurrection*, 2, 4; see also Martyn Smith, *Religion, Culture, and Sacred Space* (New York: Palgrave MacMillan, 2008), 53–4.

[77] Smith, *Religion, Culture, and Sacred Space*, 54–55.

[78] Herodotus II:63; Cary, trans., 119.

6. Various purification rites inside the temple of the god to close out the festival

The stele of Ikhernefert also preserves some intriguing hints about Ikhernefert's other activities with respect to establishing Osiris's new temple. Apparently Ikhernefert had been charged with reforming the worship of Osiris in addition to his construction work, since he claims to have instructed "the hour priests of the temple so that they might do their duties and know the rituals that pertain to each day and the festivals at the start of the seasons."[79]

In addition to presiding over the Tuat and judging the souls of the dead, Osiris was inextricably linked with fertility. In ancient Egypt, this meant being linked with the yearly flood cycle of the Nile, which continued into the twentieth century CE until the construction of dams and a system of canals along the river put a stop to the inundations. Prior to modern times, the Nile's yearly flood cycle began around the middle of August when monsoons that began the previous May in the Ethiopian highlands dumped an enormous quantity of water into the Nile and other rivers in the area. The swollen river would rise through the end of August and reach its peak in September, after which it would begin to recede, leaving a layer of enormously fertile sediment behind. The receding of the flood reached its lowest point in April, and in the following August, the cycle would begin again.

For the ancient Egyptians, the annual floods were integral not only to the agricultural calendar but also to the religious one, which connected the flood itself and the fecundity it promoted to the person of and myths about Osiris. In his role as a god of fertility, Osiris was linked with the life cycle of grain crops, the success of which was bound up with the cycle of floods. Ancient Egyptians believed that just as Osiris died and came back to life twice, so too did the seed "die" when it was sown only to rise back up and be cut down again at

---

[79] Translation in Smith, *Religion, Culture, and Sacred Space*, 53.

harvest time, when it would "die" again through being transformed into food products such as bread and beer.[80] Worshipers would even make little effigies of the mummified Osiris, stuffed with seeds, which they would then plant and tend. However, not only was the grain that grew from the Nile's muddy bounty aligned with Osiris, but as Veronica Ions states, the floodwaters themselves were also considered to be the "sweat of Osiris's hands and the tears that Isis shed into the river."[81]

The myth of Osiris's death and subsequent resurrection has led some scholars to attempt to show a direct line of descent between ancient Egyptian religion and Christianity, the latter of which centers around the death and resurrection of Jesus of Nazareth. However, scholarly opinion is divided as to whether this lineage exists. The death and resurrection stories certainly would seem to run in parallel, at least up to a point. A second parallel might be that Osiris was considered to be somehow embodied in the grain consumed by his followers, while according to some Christian sects, Jesus's essence is said to be contained in the eucharistic bread because of the words of institution—"this is my body"—uttered at the Last Supper.[82] And Jesus is seen as a guide and savior who can restore the souls of the dead to an everlasting life that is open to all people, regardless of station, a role he shares with Osiris.

Whether there is an actual organic connection between the Osiris cult and the establishment of Christianity remains an open question, but the adaptation and transformation of the Osiris cult within the context of Egyptian religion during the Ptolemaic Period in Egypt is not. Osiris was combined with the Apis bull by Ptolemy I into a new deity known as Serapis, and the worship of Osiris as a god in his own right gradually faded out, although rites were still being performed at

---

[80] Henri Frankfort, *Ancient Egyptian Religion: An Interpretation* (New York: Harper & Row, 1948), 28.

[81] Ions, *Egyptian Mythology*, 108.

[82] Mark 14:22-25; Luke 22:18-20.

the temple complex in Philae until the middle of the fifth century CE, when pagan practices were outlawed in favor of Christianity.

As was the case in Hellenized Egypt, Osiris has received less attention than Isis and Thoth from modern occultists and pagans, although scholarly interest in Osiris as a god of death and resurrection became renewed during the late nineteenth century, when Sir James George Frazer published *The Golden Bough*, a comparative study of world religions.[83] In that study, Frazer connected Osiris with other gods such as Tammuz/Dumuzi, an ancient Mesopotamian god, and Attis, a Phrygian deity. However, scholars have since disputed many of Frazer's claims, stating that they are not supported by the evidence.[84]

---

[83] James George Frazer, *The Golden Bough: A Study in Magic and Religion*, third ed. Part IV, Vol. 11, *Adonis Attis Osiris* (London: The MacMillan Press, Ltd., 1914).

[84] See, for example, Paul Rhodes Eddy and Gregory A. Boyd, *The Jesus Legend: A Case for the Historical Reliability of the Synoptic Jesus Tradition* (Grand Rapids: Baker Academic, 2007), 143.

Ptah

The supreme god of the city of Memphis was Ptah. In the Memphite cosmogony, Ptah is the creator god from whom all other gods spring at the beginning of creation. First, Ptah (who is also identified with Nun, the primeval waters) creates Atum, and then Atum goes on to create the Ennead, a collection of nine gods worshiped primarily at Heliopolis. Ptah also creates the world and sets the land of Egypt in order. Some scholars think that the elevation of Ptah to supreme creator might have been an attempt on the part of his priests in Memphis to create a hierarchy in which the chief gods of Heliopolis were made subordinate to Memphis's own.[85]

Ptah is usually depicted as a man wearing a tight skullcap and straight beard. He holds the *was* scepter, which was the symbol of power and authority in Egypt. This scepter has two small horns at its foot and a hook with a kind of antler at the top. Some images of Ptah show his body swathed tightly in the linen wrappings of a mummy, with green skin on his face and hands. Ptah's consort is the lion-headed goddess Sekhmet, and their son is Nefertem, who was said to have originated as a lotus flower and who was associated with fragrance and perfumes.

---

[85] Hart, *Dictionary*, 129.

Ptah was the patron of craftsmen in ancient Egypt. Egyptologist George Hart reports that images of craftsmen praying to Ptah survive on stelae at what is now Deir el-Medina. These stelae were made by the workers who did sculpting work for tombs in the Valley of the Kings.[86] This connection between Ptah and craftsmanship perhaps reached its peak in the person of Imhotep, who served during the Third Dynasty as the master sculptor to Pharaoh Djoser, and who may have been the architect of Djoser's step pyramid. Imhotep's reputation for wisdom and integrity eventually led him to be deified, at which point he was often referred to as the "son of Ptah." (See the chapter on Imhotep above.)

---

[86] Hart, *Dictionary*, 130-31.

Ra (Re, Pre)

Ra was the Egyptian god of the sun, an all-powerful creator who rode in the Barque of Millions of Years across the sky each day to bring light and life to the earth. At night, the barque descended into the Underworld, where Ra and his crew had to brave various dangers in order to get to the other side so that the sun might rise again in the morning. The chief enemy of Ra was the great serpent Apep (Apophis), who had to be slain each night. Ra's chief cult center was in the city of Heliopolis, and he eventually became identified with the creator god Atum. Egyptologist Leonard Lesko observes that Ra's cult was so influential and powerful that it eventually appropriated both the Heliopolitan and Hermopolitan cosmologies, integrating them into the mythology about Ra's origins, powers, and role within the pantheon.[87]

One example of this association with the Heliopolitan cosmology comes from the *Book of the Dead*. In that text, Atum, the primary god of the Heliopolitan Ennead, is the manifestation of the creator at the beginning of creation, just following his emergence from the

---

[87] Leonard H. Lesko, "Ancient Egyptian Cosmogonies and Cosmology," in *Religion in Ancient Egypt: Gods, Myths, and Personal Practice*, ed. by Byron E. Shafer (Ithaca: Cornell University Press, 1991), 115.

primordial waters, while Ra is his manifestation in the person of the sun god and as the sun itself.[88] In creation myths, therefore, Atum and Ra become interchangeable versions of the same deity.

Ra also had multiple forms in his manifestation as the sun. Ra-Horakhty represented the sun at midday, while Ra-Atum was the setting sun and Khepera the rising sun in the morning. Each of these forms had their own visual representations. Khepera was the scarab beetle, who pushed the sun above the horizon in much the same way that these beetles push balls of dung around. Ra-Horakhty was pictured as a man with a falcon's head, and Ra-Atum was pictured as a human man wearing the double crown of Egypt. In addition, Ra was sometimes said to become Osiris at night, when he traveled through the Underworld.

Although each of these representations show a male figure, the manifestation of Ra's power, the Eye of Ra, was conceived of as female. The Eye was both part of Ra and separate from him. He could detach it and send it to do his bidding, and when he did so, it was in the form of a goddess, such as Hathor or Sekhmet. We see this in the myth in which Ra decides to destroy all of humanity because they are leading evil lives and not worshiping the gods properly. To achieve this, Ra sends his Eye in the form of Hathor (who is also Sekhmet) to kill all the people and to ravage their lands. Because the Eye was separate from Ra, he did not always exercise full control over it. In the "Distant Goddess" myth, Ra's Eye (again in the form of a goddess such as Hathor) runs away into the desert and has to be fetched back and reunited with Ra.

The living embodiment of the *ba*, or spirit, of Ra was the Mnevis bull, a sacred bull that was kept at the temple of Ra in Heliopolis. This animal was usually all black, and had two cows to serve as his wives. The cows were said to represent the goddesses Hathor, who often functioned as the Eye of Ra, and Iusas, a goddess said to be the

---

[88] Lesko, "Cosmogonies and Cosmology," 113.

hand of Atum that worked to produce the seed from which all creation was made. When the Mnevis bull died, it was mummified and buried with great ceremony. Egyptologist Barbara Watterson notes that the Mnevis bull remained a popular and important aspect of the worship of Ra well into the Ptolemaic Period.[89]

In some myths, Ra is portrayed as weak and old, or else as vacillating, peevish, and unwilling to say aloud what he really believes. In the story about how Isis learned Ra's true name, Ra is described as an incontinent old man who has lost all of his teeth, and Isis tortures him with venomous snake bites until he relents and tells her his name. In "The Battle of Horus and Set," Ra-Horakhty is the king of the gods, but when the matter at hand isn't settled either quickly or to his liking, he goes off into his tent to sulk. Further, Ra-Horakhty supports Set's claim to the throne, but will not come forth to order that Set be given the crown; in fact, he is described as secretly supporting Set over Horus. In this tale, Ra-Horakhty lacks the courage of his convictions, and he proposes several maneuvers intended to get others to make the decision for him.

Ra was often syncretized with other deities. Amen-Ra was one especially important syncretization in the New Kingdom. Other syncretizations included Sobek-Ra and Khnum-Ra.

---

[89] Watterson, *Gods of Ancient Egypt*, 68.

Serapis (Sarapis, Userhapi)

Unlike the other gods in the Egyptian pantheon, Serapis was not a product of the native Egyptian religious imagination. Serapis did not grow out of the native Egyptian understanding of the world or its origins, nor was he allied to native Egyptian ideas about social and political structures. Instead, Serapis was a deity purpose-built by Ptolemy I, the Greek successor to Alexander the Great, who wished to find some way to fuse Greek and Egyptian religious expression and so lend legitimacy to the rule of Egypt by her Greek conquerors.

Serapis was in part a syncretization of the god Osiris and the Apis bull. The Apis bull was worshiped particularly in Memphis, where he was said to be the son of Hathor and the herald of Ptah, and where he was a symbol of the ruling pharaoh. Worship of the Apis bull had been a feature of Egyptian religion at least since the First Dynasty, and the worship of Osiris became commonplace during the Fifth, so both were already well entrenched in the Egyptian pantheon by the time the Ptolemies came to power.

In addition to this syncretization of ancient Egyptian deities, Ptolemy tacked Greek characteristics onto Serapis to round out the new god's appeal to both Greeks and Egyptians. For example, when images of Serapis were made, they were constructed along the same lines as other contemporary Greek representations of religious and political figures. Serapis therefore is depicted realistically as a muscular adult male with long curly hair and a beard, often with a basket on top of his head, and he shared certain features with Greek gods such as Zeus, Dionysus, and Hades.

This association with Hades, who in Rome was known as Pluto, is attested to in the writings of the ancient historian Plutarch, who also states that Serapis was brought to Egypt by Ptolemy I as the result of a dream.[90] In the dream, the statue of Pluto at Sinope tells Ptolemy to take him from Sinope and bring him to Alexandria. The statue supposedly included a representation of Pluto's three-headed dog Cerberus. Plutarch goes on to say that when the statue arrived in Alexandria, Ptolemy declared it to be a representation of Serapis.

In order to form the traditional Egyptian triad, Serapis was said to be the husband of Isis and the father of Horus. The form of Horus used was that of Harpocrates, the winged child deity who was the god of secrets and who had already found favor among Greek worshipers. Although the Egyptian priests in Heliopolis attempted to integrate Serapis into their religious thought by positing that Serapis was created when the soul of the Apis bull entered the afterlife and merged with Osiris, Serapis never really found much favor among the native Egyptian populace, who preferred to worship their own traditional gods.[91]

Serapis was much more popular outside of Egypt, especially in Rome. In Rome, Serapis was worshiped alongside Isis, who had a temple that had been built by Emperor Caligula in the Campus Martius, an important area in ancient Rome that housed public baths and the temple known as the Pantheon, which is still intact and may be visited today.

---

[90] C. W. King, trans. *Plutarch's Morals: Theosophical Essays* (London: George Bell & Sons, 1889), 22–23.

[91] Ions, *Egyptian Mythology*, 122.

The Roman emperor Vespasian particularly seems to have made use of the power attributed to Serapis in order to boost his own popularity and authority, particularly within Egypt, which at that time was part of the Roman Empire. The ancient historian Tacitus reports that while Vespasian was visiting Alexandria, a blind man and a man with a disabled hand came to Vespasian saying that Serapis had sent them to the emperor to be healed.[92] At first Vespasian scoffed at this, but then he did what the two disabled men asked, and they were healed. According to Tacitus, Vespasian then made it a point to go to the Serapeum, or temple to Serapis, where he ordered everyone else to leave so that he might consult the god alone. There Vespasian had a vision, which he considered to have been sent by Serapis himself.

Serapis was of sufficient importance in imperial Rome that he often was depicted on coins. Coinage from the reigns of Vespasian and some later emperors feature the face of the emperor in profile on one side and an image of Serapis, sometimes accompanied by Isis, on the other.

---

[92] Cornelius Tacitus, *The Works of Tacitus: The Oxford Translation, Revised*, vol. 2: *The History, Germany, Agricola, and Dialogue on Orations* (New York: Harper & Brothers, Publishers, 1858),

Set (Seth, Sutekh)

Set is one of the oldest Egyptian gods, having been worshiped in the Predynastic Period. Set also is an ambivalent character, representing both good and evil. Whether his role is good or bad depends partly on the time period and partly on the activity in which Set is engaged at the time. He was the murderer of his brother Osiris and a pretender to the throne of Egypt, but he also rode in the prow of the solar barge and killed Apep, the giant serpent that threatened to devour the sun every night.

The god of chaos, thunder, and deserts, Set is depicted as a man with the head of a strange animal that has never been definitively identified. The Set-animal is black in color, with a long, narrow snout and two upright, rectangular ears. Some scholars have said that the Set-animal is a composite creature made up of parts from other animals, while others have suggested that it might represent a type of dog resembling the modern Saluki.

In Egyptian myth, Set is depicted as jealous and ruthless, willing to murder, maim, and rape in order to get his way. By the New Kingdom, Set is also depicted as being more brawn than brain; we see this especially in the story "The Battle of Horus and Set," where he is easily fooled by Horus and Isis, who are just as willing to cheat as Set is.

Perhaps the most famous story in which Set appears is that of Isis and Osiris. In this story, which is variously summarized in the above chapters on the latter two deities, Set contrives to murder Osiris not once but twice in order to steal his throne. In the second instance, Set dismembers Osiris, and because Osiris's penis is consumed by a fish, Osiris will never be whole again, despite the heroic efforts of Isis, Anubis, Thoth, and other deities who work together to resurrect him.

In the story in which Set contends with Horus for the throne, summarized in the chapter on Horus above, Set is unwilling to accept the judgment of the court of the gods, and proposes various contests between himself and Horus to see who ought to have the throne of Egypt. Neither contest is ever decided in favor of one or the other, because Horus and his mother Isis try to cheat and thus skew the results. Set, on the other hand, for all that he may be murderous and rather stupid, tries to follow the rules when he accepts these challenges.

Rules go out the window, however, when Set sees an opportunity to discredit Horus first by attempting to rape him and then by trying to shame him by saying publicly that the sex was consensual. This trick backfires when Set ends up ejaculating into Horus's hands. Horus then enlists the help of his mother to show that Set was lying about what actually happened. Set likewise takes advantage of an opportunity to maim Horus while the latter is sleeping and therefore defenseless, but Horus is eventually restored to health by Hathor.

Early in Egyptian history, Set was worshiped primarily in Upper Egypt, where he had a cult center at Kom Ombo. Set later was worshiped throughout the country, and several pharaohs had a particular devotion to him. Eventually, however, Set began to be seen more as a force for evil and fell out of favor. Egyptologist Geraldine Pinch reports that starting in the New Kingdom, Egyptian religion began to concentrate more on Set's crimes, such that the priests of

Horus at Edfu "celebrated a day of castrating Seth and 'reducing him to pieces' in retaliation for Seth's mutilation of the body of Osiris and the Eye of Horus."[93] The process of demonizing Set continued from the New Kingdom onward and, as Pinch states, reached its peak during the Greco-Roman period, at which point, "Seth was vilified in most temples."[94]

---

[93] Pinch, *Handbook*, 193.
[94] Pinch, *Handbook*, 193.

Sobek (Suchos)

The crocodile-headed Sobek was a god of the waters and of fertility and the son of the mother goddess Neith. Sobek originally was a deity specific to the Fayum region, which in ancient times was a marshy oasis, located about sixty miles south of what is now Cairo. During the Twelfth Dynasty, pharaohs such as Amenemhat III worked to harness the water of the Fayum region by creating a canal from the Nile into Lake Moeris, which seems to have been used as a kind of reservoir that could be drawn on in times of drought. The chief settlement in the Fayum in ancient times was Shedet, known in Greek as Crocodilopolis.

Crocodiles are native to the Nile, and since ancient Egyptians often associated particular animals with particular deities, it should be no surprise that a crocodile god should have been worshiped in a region known for its wetlands. Ancient temples to Sobek even kept living crocodiles as exemplars of the god. The priests cared for the animals carefully and embalmed them for proper burial when they died. Examinations of mummified adult crocodiles have even found sets of mummified babies in the mouths of the adults, likely a representation of one way in which living crocodiles care for their young. Egyptologist Salima Ikram speculates that "the insertion of babies in this manner was intented [sic] to emphasize the positive nurturing and caring aspect of this fearsome beast."[95]

In addition to his cult in the Fayum, Sobek had a major temple at Kom Ombo, which lies about halfway between Edfu and Aswan. At Kom Ombo, Sobek was revered along with Horus. Horus was given one side of the temple, while Sobek had the other, and each god was given an avatar of Hathor as his consort. Horus's son was the god Pantebtawy, "Lord of the Two Lands," while Sobek was given the moon god Khonsu to be his child.[96] However, Egyptologist Barbara Watterson notes that this combination comes with a certain amount of dissonance, as Horus's traditional enemy, the evil god Set, often took the form of a crocodile.[97] Watterson posits that the cult of Sobek at Kom Ombo was intended to be a stand-in for the worship of Set, whose cult had been outlawed.[98]

---

[95] Salima Ikram, "Protecting Pets and Cleaning Crocodiles: The Animal Mummy Project," in *Divine Creatures: Animal Mummies in Ancient Egypt*, edited by Salima Ikram (Cairo: The American University of Cairo Press, 2005), 219.

[96] Watterson, *Gods of Ancient Egypt*, 121.

[97] Watterson, *Gods of Ancient Egypt*, 121.

[98] Watterson, *Gods of Ancient Egypt*, 122.

Thoth

In Egyptian mythology, Thoth held a position of great importance as the creator of writing and law, and as the god who oversaw the calendar and ordered the times and the seasons. Today, many people are familiar with the depiction of Thoth as a man with the head of an ibis, but in ancient Egypt he was also depicted in the form of a baboon, sometimes with a lunar disk over its head and sometimes without. As with other Egyptian deities, Thoth was adopted by devotees from outside of Egypt, eventually becoming syncretized with the Greek messenger god Hermes. Thoth's association with magic and knowledge also attracted the interest of alchemists, magicians, and occultists in both the Renaissance and in more modern times.

There is no single myth describing Thoth's origins. Depending on the source, he is variously said to have emerged into being through his own power or to have been spoken into being by the sun god Ra. In the former myth, Thoth is also the creator of the universe, an act that he accomplishes in his ibis-form by laying the egg from which all matter and all being is hatched at the beginning of time.

These varying conceptions of Thoth and his origins arise both from changes in Egyptian religious thought across time and also from regional differences in religious practices. In the city of Memphis, the supreme god was Ptah, and Thoth was conceptualized as both the tongue and the wisdom of Ptah.[99] The myth of the egg mentioned above, by contrast, comes from the city of Hermopolis, and may have been a later addition to religious doctrine and practice there.[100] Indeed, the very name of Hermopolis is a reference to Thoth. The original Egyptian name was Khemenu, a reference to the Ogdoad, or Eight Gods, that were worshiped in that city, but when Egypt was Hellenized, the name was changed to Hermopolis, which literally means "City of Hermes" in Greek. This change came about because of the syncretization of the Greek god Hermes with Thoth and because of the central importance of Thoth to Egyptian religious practice in Hermopolis.

In all parts of Egypt, Thoth was considered to be a lunar god. One myth explains that Thoth acquired his association with the moon when the heavily pregnant goddess Nut asked him for help in reversing the curse placed on her by Ra, who had told her that she would not be able to give birth during any day on the calendar, which at that time had 360 days. Thoth solves the problem by gambling with the moon god Khonsu, setting the stakes at a fifth of Khonsu's light. When Thoth wins the contest, he uses Khonsu's light to create five intercalary days, during which Nut is finally able to give birth to Osiris, Horus, Set, Isis, and Nephthys. In this myth, we also see Thoth's role as a god of time and the calendar, since it is his bet with Khonsu that allows the calendar to be expanded from the lunar 360 days to the solar 365. Thoth therefore is responsible for ensuring that the seasons and the calendar remain aligned.

Thoth was credited with inventing the art of writing, and in this capacity he was especially revered by the scribes of ancient Egypt. Because of this association with words and writing, Thoth was depicted as the recorder of human deeds who stood with Anubis

---

[99] Ions, *Egyptian Mythology*, 28.
[100] Ions, *Egyptian Mythology*, 29.

beside the scales that weighed human hearts after death in order to determine the soul's ultimate eternal fate. In other contexts, Thoth uses his skills with writing and his wisdom to function as a scribe, herald, and judge for the supreme god Ra and the other deities. We see this in the New Kingdom myth "The Battle of Horus and Set," summarized in the chapter on Horus above. When Ra desires to send letters to various gods and goddesses, it is Thoth who takes dictation from Ra and sends the letters. In this story, Thoth also makes performative proclamations instituting the commands of various deities. When Thoth makes statements such as "Let this thing be done!" he functions both as a judge who determines whether laws are to be enacted and as a herald who announces the start of a new law.

During the Ptolemaic Period, Thoth was absorbed into Greek and Roman religion, where he was syncretized with the Greek god Hermes, as mentioned earlier, and with the Roman god Mercury. Like Thoth, Hermes was associated with writing and was considered to be the messenger or herald of the Olympian gods. Thoth also acquired Hermes's role as the guide of souls into the Underworld, and became known as "Hermes Trismegistus," or "Thrice-Great Hermes."

As Hermes Trismegistus, Thoth was credited with having written a series of books on magic, known collectively as the *Corpus Hermeticum*, or "Body of Works by Hermes." These texts were, in fact, written by an anonymous human author during the second century CE and not by Thoth himself, but the association with the god granted the *Corpus* a certain cachet among magicians and seekers after truth. The *Corpus* was also incredibly important to Renaissance and Early Modern magicians and was a focal text in the practice of alchemy, a magical science that laid some of the important groundwork for modern chemistry.

Interest in Thoth's magic was revived in the late nineteenth and early twentieth centuries by groups such as the Hermetic Order of the Golden Dawn, a secret group interested in magic and the occult whose membership included Irish revolutionary Maud Gonne and authors Sir Arthur Conan Doyle, W. B. Yeats, and Bram Stoker. One other member of the Order was the occultist Aleister Crowley, whose *Book of Thoth* is an essay on the history and uses of the tarot deck that draws on aspects of various ancient religions and mythologies, including those of Egypt. Crowley especially connects Thoth with the tarot figure of the Juggler (also known in the modern tarot as the Magician), which Crowley considered to be aligned with Mercury, both the planet and the Roman god.

The Tuat (Duat)

The Tuat was the ancient Egyptian Underworld, and it had multiple functions within Egyptian religion and culture. Some functions were cosmological, but most of them related to beliefs about death and to funerary practices. The Tuat was the place where people initially went when they died. It was the domain of Osiris, and it was where the hearts of the dead were weighed to see whether they were pure and clean and thus worthy of paradise or not. The Tuat was also the place that the sun god had to traverse each night as he went from west to east to begin a new day, and it was the place to which the stars descended when their season in the sky was done.

For both human beings and the sun god Ra, the Tuat was a conduit to rebirth, not a final resting place. Ancient Egyptians believed that when the sun descended below the western horizon at night, it entered into the Tuat. When the sun god entered the Tuat as Atum-Ra, the body of the god was separated from his *ba*, or soul, and the body was cast aside and discarded. The sun god therefore needed to be united with a new body and rejuvenated before he could rise again in the east as Khepera, the scarab beetle who pushed the sun up into the sky out of the waters of Nun.

The sun's barge was sometimes known as the Atet boat or the Barque of Millions of Years, but when it went into the Underworld, it was renamed the Meseket boat or Sektet boat. Because there was no wind in the Tuat, the barge had to be rowed or towed along the path between the western entrance and the eastern exit. The work of towing or rowing was done by different sets of deities, depending on where along the path the boat happened to be at the moment. The sun god was always a passenger, and only helped with the journey by speaking to the different beings encountered in the Tuat.

When a human being died, their soul went down into the Tuat, where it had to make its way to the place where the god Anubis weighed the hearts of the dead. If the heart of the dead person was found to be pure and good, the person would leave the Tuat and go to the Field of Reeds, which was the Egyptian paradise. In the Field of Reeds, the dead person was reunited with their body, and they continued to live in much the same way as they had done before death, only without pain, disease, hunger, or hard work. If the heart was found to be evil, however, the soul was devoured by Ammit and destroyed forever, never to be reunited with the body.

The ancient Egyptian fascination with the Tuat and the afterlife is manifest in the hundreds of surviving funerary texts that describe the Tuat's hazards, denizens, and geographical features. Such texts also provided spells and other information the soul of the dead person would need to navigate the dangers of the Tuat. At first, funerary texts were written only in the tombs of the pharaohs, because it was believed that only the pharaoh was able to go on to paradise and live forever. Later, this privilege was accorded to the nobility, but eventually any Egyptian person was thought to be eligible for resurrection and eternal life in the Field of Reeds. This doctrinal change created a market for funerary texts, which would be buried with the mummified body for the use of the dead person as they made their way across the Tuat.

Funerary texts became available to anyone with the funds to purchase them starting in the New Kingdom. Two of the most important texts were the *Book of the Dead* and the *Amduat*. The latter is a lavishly illustrated book whose title literally means "what is in the Underworld," and it gives a detailed description of the sun's nighttime journey. The *Book of the Dead*, by contrast, is less a description of the Underworld than a practical guide to how to get through it.

According to the *Amduat*, the Tuat was divided into twelve regions, with each region representing one of the twelve hours of the night. Each region has its own geographical features and is inhabited by its own set of deities, some of whom temporarily join Ra's crew in order to get his barge from one end of the region to the other. One such deity who is aboard only through a particular region is called the "Lady of the Boat"; her duty is to protect Ra and his barge while it is in her territory. In addition to deities and various physical features, some regions also have hazards that need to be negotiated. The solar barge itself undergoes changes depending on where it happens to be at the moment. For example, the mummified Ra is usually seated either in an open space in the middle of the boat or else under a kind of tent, but at one point a friendly giant serpent comes aboard and forms a new tent with its body to protect Ra on that part of his journey.

Below are highly abbreviated descriptions of the twelve regions according to the *Amduat*:[101]

1. In one illustration for this region, the sun god stands in the middle of the barge in his *ba*-form as a ram-headed man with a solar

---

[101] Synopsis based on E. A. Wallace Budge, *The Egyptian Heaven and Hell*, vol. 1: *The Book Am-Tuat* (London: Kegan Paul, Trench, Trübner & Co., Ltd., 1905); Erik Hornung, *The Ancient Egyptian Books of the Afterlife*, trans. David Lorton (Ithaca: Cornell University Press, 1999), 33–53; and Remler, *Egyptian Mythology A to Z*, 9.

disk between his horns; in another, he is shown as a scarab beetle. Egyptologist Erik Hornung states that this is intended to show that the sun's journey is expected to be completed successfully.[102] Nine baboons in this region have the job of opening the gates of the Tuat so that the solar barge can go through, while another nine sing to Ra. Because the sun is dead and has no light at this point, there are magical serpents who provide light in this region. Various other deities praise the sun god, who asks permission to enter the Tuat proper. Permission is granted, and the baboons open the doors.

2. Still in his ram-headed form (which with one exception he will keep until the end of the journey), the sun god rides in his barge along a stream. Several rowers propel the barge. Isis and Nephthys are aboard in the form of serpents. Ra's boat is accompanied by several other barges at this stage. One is the barge of the moon, another is the barge of Hathor, a third is occupied by a god in lizard form, and the last is the boat of Neper, the god of grain, who is an avatar of Osiris. Many other gods and goddesses are in this region as well, who praise Ra and ask him to renew himself. Ra replies with blessings for the denizens of the region and a command that evil beings be banished. He then asks for help in his journey across the Tuat.

---

[102] Hornung, *Books of the Afterlife*, 34.

3. The barge is rowed along with ram-headed Ra in the middle. As in the second region, there are four other boats on the river with the solar barge. The first is called "the boat that capsizes," and it carries Horus deities. The second and third boats are called "the boat of rest" and "the boat of the branch," respectively. Each carries a mummified Osiris. In addition to the main deity, each of these subsidiary boats have a crew of other gods and goddesses. Mummified forms of Osiris appear elsewhere in the illustrations for this region as well.

4. In the fourth region, water does not flow. The barge instead has to be towed over sand, and it is a different barge from the one in the first three regions, having serpents' heads at the prow and stern. The fourth region is called the "region of Sokar." Sokar (or Seker) was the Memphite god of the dead. Snakes slither over the sand here, and instead of moving straight across the page, the solar boat now takes a downward path, which goes from the upper right corner to the lower left. One part of the illustration shows two gods guarding the Eye of Ra. In Wallace Budge's edition of the book, these gods are Thoth and Horus. The winged sun disk appears in this region as well, as does the goddess Maat.

5. Still in the region of Sokar, Ra's boat continues its descent, this time moving diagonally downward from the upper left corner to the lower right. The burial mound

of Osiris is here, watched over by Isis and Nephthys, who are in bird-form as kites. Ra makes various addresses to the beings who live in this region, asking that he be allowed to pass through unmolested.

6. Ra switches to a barge that floats on the water and is paddled by a crewman. Erik Hornung states that this water is the water of Nun.103 There are four sets of mummified beings, and each set represents the kings of a different cardinal direction. The dead body of Ra is represented by a recumbent man holding the scarab of Khepera over his head, encircled by an enormous serpent. According to Hornung, it is in this region that the dead body of the sun is conceptualized as the dead body of Osiris, which here is reunited with its ba, represented by the scarab.

7. The seventh region is called the "Hall of Osiris." Ra is once again depicted as a ram-headed man with the solar disk between his horns, but instead of the usual canopy, he is now covered by an arch made by the giant serpent Mehen. Mehen will continue to protect Ra in this way until Ra is reborn as Khepera and rises as the new sun. Isis stands in the prow with her arms outstretched, using her magic to make the boat move. The giant serpent Apophis is shown having been defeated; his body is pierced by six knives, while a goddess strangles him near his head

---

[103] Hornung, *Books of the Afterlife*, 37.

and a god ties up his tail. A form of Horus also appears in this region, in the form of a seated man with a hawk's head, on which is the solar disk to which a uraeus is attached. It is Horus's job to make the stars rise and to see to it that time continues to flow. Twelve gods represent the stars, while twelve goddesses represent the hours of the day and night.

8. In this region, Mehen's power gives the crew towing the barge the ability to make progress across the waters. There are four rams depicted here, each with a different headdress. The rams represent manifestations of Tatanen, the god of the primordial mound from which creation arose. Several other deities are depicted along with looms and other things needed to weave cloth. Of these representations of weaving, Erik Hornung observes that "[t]he theme of this hour is thus the supplying of clothes, which from early times on represented a high priority among the things wished for in the afterlife."[104]

9. One section of the illustrations for this region shows the twelve gods who row Ra's barge. The other job these gods have is to use their paddles to splash water onto the riverbank for the use of the spirits who dwell there. Ra also promises to provide food and drink for the beings who live in this region. Besides the crew of the barge, there are

---

[104] Hornung, *Books of the Afterlife*, 39.

twelve goddesses who sing praises to Osiris, and twelve fire-breathing uraei who use their power to protect Ra as he passes by.

10. Ra continues to stand under the arch of Mehen's body, but now he carries an ankh in his right hand, while his left holds a staff in the shape of a serpent. A series of illustrations show four gods holding spears, four holding arrows, and four holding bows. Ra bids these gods destroy his enemies with their weapons. The spirits of those who have drowned dwell in the waters here; Ra promises that they can enter paradise even though they haven't been mummified. It is in the tenth region that Ra and Khepera are joined together in preparation for sunrise. This is represented in part by an illustration of a scarab beetle pushing an elliptical shape that represents the horizon. Thoth, in his baboon manifestation, holds the Eye of Horus so that it can be healed by the goddess Sekhmet.

11. The text for this region states that the deities who live here are guiding the sun to the eastern horizon so that he can rise again. Ra rides in his boat covered by Mehen, but elsewhere in this section, Mehen appears as an enormously long snake being carried along by twelve gods who go on foot. Their job is to see to it that Mehen also arrives safely at the eastern horizon. A fourfold manifestation of the goddess Neith is to be found here, as are a series of pits of fire in which the enemies of

Ra are consumed. Each pit has its own attendant deity tending the flames.

12. After a long and dangerous journey, Ra's solar barge finally arrives at the eastern horizon. Ram-headed Ra stands in the middle of the boat under his Mehen-canopy, while Khepera occupies the prow in the form of a scarab. One portion of the text in Budge's translation reads: "Then this great god taketh up his position in the Eastern Horizon of heaven, and Shu receiveth him, and he cometh into being in the East."105 But before sunrise can happen, Ra's barge has to travel the length of a giant serpent named Ankhneteru. For this part of the journey, the barge is towed by twelve gods and twelve goddesses. The goddesses towing the barge also have the duty of creating breezes on earth. Twelve additional goddesses carry fire-breathing serpents on their shoulders. The serpents use their fire to repel the enemies of Ra, especially the demon serpent Apophis. Another twelve gods sing praises to Ra. The final illustration shows a curved wall at the rightmost edge of the papyrus. This represents the horizon. The god Khepera, in the form of a scarab beetle, pushes the sun disk through the middle of the wall. The disk is placed beneath the head of the air god Shu, whose arms extend along the inner perimeter of the wall. At the bottom of the wall is a mummy representing Ra's night body, which

---

[105] Budge, *Am-Tuat*, 258.

he has cast off and which will be destroyed now that he has been born again as the rising sun.

Here's another book by Captivating History that you might be interested in

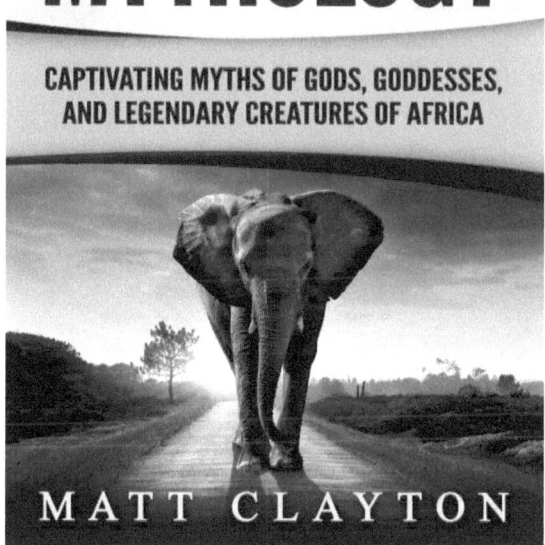

Bibliography

Allen, James P. *The Ancient Egyptian Pyramid Texts.* Atlanta: Society of Biblical Literature, 2005.

Bricault, Laurent. *Isis Pelagia: Images, Names and Cults of a Goddess of the Seas.* Trans. Gil H. Renberg. Leiden: Brill, 2020.

Budge, E. A. Wallace. *Osiris and the Egyptian Resurrection.* 2 vols. London: P. L. Warner, [1911].

———. *The Book of Opening the Mouth: The Egyptian Texts With English Translations.* 2 vols. London: Kegan Paul, Trench, Trübner & Co., Ltd., 1909.

———. *The Egyptian Heaven and Hell.* Vol. 1: *The Book Am-Tuat.* London: Kegan Paul, Trench, Trübner & Co., Ltd., 1905.

Bunson, Margaret. *Encyclopedia of Ancient Egypt.* Rev. ed. New York: Facts on File, Inc., 2010.

Cary, Henry, trans. *Herodotus.* London: George Bell and Sons, 1901.

Crowley, Aleister. *The Book of Thoth.* Repr. York Beach: Samuel Weiser, Inc., 1995.

David, A. Rosalie. *Discovering Ancient Egypt.* New York: Facts on File, Inc., 1994.

———. *The Ancient Egyptians: Religious Beliefs and Practices.* London: Routledge & Kegan Paul, 1982.

Eddy, Paul Rhodes, and Gregory A. Boyd. *The Jesus Legend: A Case for the Historical Reliability of the Synoptic Jesus Tradition.* Grand Rapids: Baker Academic, 2007.

Ellis, Normandi. *Feasts of Light: Celebrations for the Seasons of Life Based on the Egyptian Goddess Mysteries.* Wheaton: The Theosophical Publishing House, 1999.

Escolano-Poveda, Marina. "Imhotep: A Sage Between Fiction and Reality." American Research Center in Egypt website, accessed 23 June 2020, https://www.arce.org/resource/imhotep-sage-between-fiction-and-reality.

Forty, Jo. *Ancient Egyptian Mythology.* Edison: Chartwell Books, Inc., 1996.

Frankfort, Henri. *Ancient Egyptian Religion.* New York: Harper & Row, 1948.

Frazer, James George. *The Golden Bough: A Study in Magic and Religion,* Part IV, Vol. 2, 3rd ed., *Adonis Attis Osiris.* London: The MacMillan Press, Ltd., 1914.

Graves-Brown, Carolyn. *Dancing for Hathor: Women in Ancient Egypt.* London: Continuum, 2010.

Griffiths, John Gwyn. *The Origins of Osiris and his Cult.* Leiden: Brill, 1980.

Hart, George. *A Dictionary of Egyptian Gods and Goddesses.* London: Routledge, 2000.

Heyob, Sharon Kelly. *The Cult of Isis Among Women in the Graeco-Roman World.* Leiden: E. J. Brill, 1975.

Hollis, Susan Tower. *Five Egyptian Goddesses: Their Possible Beginnings, Actions, and Relationships in the Third Millennium BCE.* n.c.: Bloomsbury Publishing, 2019.

Hornung, Erik. *The Ancient Egyptian Books of the Afterlife*. Trans. David Lorton. Ithaca: Cornell University Press, 1999.

Ikram, Salima. "Protecting Pets and Cleaning Crocodiles: The Animal Mummy Project." In *Divine Creatures: Animal Mummies in Ancient Egypt*. Edited by Salima Ikram, 207-27. Cairo: The American University in Cairo Press, 2005.

Ions, Veronica. *Egyptian Mythology*. New York: Peter Bedrick Books, 1990.

Jackson, Leslie. *Isis: The Eternal Goddess of Egypt and Rome*. London: Avalonia, 2016.

King, C. W., trans. *Plutarch's Morals: Theosophical Essays*. London: George Bell & Sons, 1889.

Kramer, Samuel Noah. *Mythologies of the Ancient World*. Garden City: Doubleday, 1961.

Lesko, Leonard H. "Ancient Egyptian Cosmogonies and Cosmology." In *Religion in Ancient Egypt: Gods, Myths, and Personal Practice*, edited by Byron E. Shafer, 90-121. Ithaca. Cornell University Press, 1991.

Lichtheim, Miriam. *Ancient Egyptian Literature: A Book of Readings*. Vol. 3, *The Late Period*. Berkeley: University of California Press, 1980.

———. *Ancient Egyptian Literature: A Book of Readings*. Vol. 2, *The New Kingdom*. Berkeley: University of California Press, 1976.

———. *Ancient Egyptian Literature: A Book of Readings*. Vol. 1, *The Old and Middle Kingdoms*. Berkeley: University of California Press, 1973.

Maehler, Herwig. "Roman Poets on Egypt." In *Ancient Perspectives on Egypt*, ed. by Roger Matthews and Cornelia Roemer, 203-15. London: UCL Press, 2003.

Mark, Joshua J. "Amun." *Ancient History Encyclopedia*, 29 July 2016, https://www.ancient.eu/amun/.

———. "Isis." *Ancient History Encyclopedia*, 19 February 2016, https://www.ancient.eu/isis/.

Martin, Luther H. *Hellenistic Religions: An Introduction.* New York: Oxford University Press 1987.

McCabe, Elizabeth A. *An Examination of the Isis Cult with Preliminary Exploration into New Testament Studies.* Lanham: University Press of America, Inc., 2008.

Mercer, Samuel A. B. *The Religion of Ancient Egypt.* London: Luzac & Co., Ltd., 1949.

Meyer, Marvin W., ed. *The Ancient Mysteries: A Sourcebook.* San Francisco: Harper & Row, 1987.

Mosjov, Bojana. *Osiris: Death and Afterlife of a God.* Malden: Blackwell Publishing, 2005.

Myśliwiec, Karol. *Eros on the Nile.* Trans. Geoffrey L. Packer. Ithaca: Cornell University Press, 1998.

Piankoff, Alexandre, trans., and Natacha Rambova, ed. *Mythological Papyri: Texts.* New York: Pantheon Books, 1957.

Pinch, Geraldine. *A Handbook of Egyptian Mythology.* Santa Barbara: ABC-CLIO, 2002.

———. *Magic in Ancient Egypt.* London: British Museum Press, 1994.

Quirke, Stephen. *Exploring Religion in Ancient Egypt.* Chichester: John Wiley & Sons, Ltd., 2010.

Regula, de Traci. *The Mysteries of Isis: Her Worship and Magick.* St. Paul: Llewellyn Publications, 2001.

Remler, Pat. *Egyptian Mythology A to Z.* 3rd ed. New York: Chelsea House, 2010.

Roth, Ann Macy. "Fingers, Stars, and the 'Opening of the Mouth': The Nature and Function of the *ntrwj*-Blades." *Journal of Egyptian Archaeology* 79 (1993): 57–79.

Simpson, William Kelley, ed. *The Literature of Ancient Egypt: An Anthology of Stories, Instructions, Stelae, Autobiographies, and Poetry.* New Haven: Yale University Press, 2003.

Smith, Mark. *Following Osiris: Perspectives on the Osirian Afterlife from Four Millennia.* Oxford: Oxford University Press, 2017.

Smith, Martyn. *Religion, Culture, and Sacred Space.* New York: Palgrave MacMillan, 2008.

Spence, Lewis. *Myths and Legends of Ancient Egypt* (Boston: David D. Nickerson & Co., [1915]).

Tacitus, Cornelius. *The Works of Tacitus: The Oxford Translation, Revised.* Vol. 2: *The History, Germany, Agricola, and Dialogue on Orations.* New York: Harper & Brothers, Publishers, 1858.

Takács, Sarolta A. *Isis and Sarapis in the Roman World.* Leiden: E. J. Brill, 1995.

Tobin, Vincent Arieh. "Isis and Demeter: Symbols of Divine Motherhood." *Journal of the American Research Center in Egypt* 28 (1991): 187–200.

Traunecker, Claude. *The Gods of Egypt.* Trans. David Lorton. Ithaca: Cornell University Press, 2001.

Tripolitis, Antonía. *Religions of the Hellenistic-Roman Age.* Grand Rapids: William B. Eerdmans Publishing Company, 2002.

Van Der Toorn, Karel, et al., eds. *Dictionary of Deities and Demons in the Bible.* 2nd ed. Leiden: Brill, 1999.

Watterson, Barbara. *The Gods of Ancient Egypt.* New York: Facts on File, Inc., 1984.

White, J. E. Manchip. *Ancient Egypt: Its Culture and History.* New York: Dover Publications, 1970.

Wildung, Dietrich. *Egyptian Saints: Deification in Pharaonic Egypt.* New York: New York University Press, 1977.

Witt, R. E. *Isis in the Ancient World*. Baltimore: Johns Hopkins University Press, 1971.